What People About This Book...

Since day one, I walked the 'Summer Adventure of 2009' with Harry, Cathy, Harrison, and the whole family. Reading *Back from Code Blue* was like reliving it in detail. I literally shed tears and had goose bumps! While the book details the harrowing journey this amazing family endured, it also depicts the immense faith, will-to-live, perseverance, support, compassion, hope, and love that surrounded them while God miraculously spared Harry's life. Cathy, your heart and soul are poured into this book, and I know it will give hope to people who need it.

Sandy Barker
Founder
Gold Rush Cure Foundation

Hope, faith, gratitude, renewed belief in God's miracles ... these are the emotions that author Cathy White infuses in us through the awe-inspiring journey of Harry's hospitalization, surgeries, and ultimate victory over death. *Back From Code Blue* strips us raw with grief, wondering how one woman could have withstood the emotional toll of those forty-four days. Then we rise, cheering each of Harry's successes over the fated "zero percent chance of surviving." Cathy and Harry lovingly bring the knowledge of heaven as home, of God's hand in our lives, from our heads to our hearts.

Chris Griffith

There are a handful of excruciatingly painful circumstances that humans sometimes endure, including the death of a child, a relative, or anyone you love deeply. Yet there is another level of this agony, experienced by a select few. It is the emotional and physical roller coaster of seeing a loved one almost die, make a recovery and appear to be "out of the woods," then relapse to "Code Blue," almost certain death, and finally by some implausible miracle, return to life.

Back From Code Blue is an odyssey of the highest highs and the lowest lows, and of trying to maintain sanity moment by moment in desperate situations. It chronicles a passage down a road that indelibly changes those who travel it. Here is a wonderful "feel good" story of that specific journey traveled by my very dear friend Dr. Harry White and his family.

I lived this story with the White family because, ironically, I had just gone through the exact same peregrination.

Jeff Reuter

I marvel at the maturity and inner strength that young Harrison exhibited throughout the entire ordeal while at the ripe old age of 14! Writing that long letter to Harry, expressing his inner most thoughts, love, devotion, and worry for his dad is something I doubt very many young people would even think to do, let alone have the wherewithal to do it.

The impact of the summer events on the White family and their many friends and acquaintances were inspirationally widespread. There isn't much greater life satisfaction than being made aware that something you said or did had a positive impact on someone's life or dream.... It doesn't happen often, but it is humbling when it does!

I firmly believe the flood of prayers got God's full attention and He graciously released Harry back to those who love him. What a tremendous miracle you were all part of. This is a wonderfully moving story of a near tragedy turned into a solid victory for God, faith, love and devotion!

~ Blaine
L. Blaine Hammond
Colonel, USAF (Retired)
Astronaut

Back from Code Blue is a high-speed roller coaster ride of raw human emotion and profoundly conflicting feelings: exhilaration and agony, joy and anguish, courage and fear, strength and frailty, resolve and self-doubt. *Code Blue* is a treasure chest of life lessons and hard-earned wisdom stitched together by Cathy from her heart-felt emails and CaringBridge posts. It is a journal that chronicles a loving wife's indomitable, relentless and irrepressible determination and courage. In the face of a 0% chance of survival, Cathy, with stubborn intransigence, refused to accept any outcome other than full recovery which based on all medical evidence, was objectively implausible if not utterly impossible.

The final take away from *Back from Code Blue* is: Believe! Nothing is impossible!

Tom Lallas

Back
From
Code Blue

By

Cathy White

HIGHERLIFE
PUBLISHING & MARKETING
Oviedo, Florida

Scripture quotations are taken from the Holy Bible, NEW INTERNATIONAL VERSION®, NIV® Copyright © 1973, 1978, 1984, 2011 by Biblica, Inc.® Used by permission. All rights reserved worldwide.

Scripture quotations noted NKJV are taken from the NEW KING JAMES VERSION, copyright 1982 by Thomas Nelson Inc. Used by permission. All rights reserved.

For permission requests, write to the publisher, addressed "Attention: Permissions Coordinator," at the address below.

Published by: HigherLife Publishing & Marketing
 PO Box 623307
 Oviedo, FL 32762
 AHigherLife.com

Photos courtesy of Cathy White.

Back from Code Blue/Cathy White -- 1st ed.

ISBN 978-1-954533-50-9 Paperback
ISBN 978-1-954533-51-6 eBook

Library of Congress Number: 2021919849

Printed in the United States of America.
10 9 8 7 6 5 4 3 2 1

This book is written in honor of
My husband, Harry,
My father-in-law, Harry, Sr.
(who passed away in 2019 at the age of 102),
And my son, Harrison.
It is also in honor of those of you who live life the way these men do,
setting examples for others of compassion, kindness, friendliness,
leaving smiles in their wakes, and making the world a better
place than it was before they arrived.

In the pre-dawn hours of July 23, 2009, life as we knew it came to an abrupt halt. It turned in a direction that would bring to mind, for most of us, the phrase, "Life is indeed stranger than fiction." "Harry's Summer Adventure of 2009," as we have come to call it, is the story of the days, weeks and months that followed that fateful day. It is a story of challenges, fortitude and forging on, of faith, support and survival; and mostly of the importance of friendship, family, positivity, and faith in God. If this story helps just one person to become more peaceful, more hopeful, more certain of his or her faith, more appreciative of the blessings of life and how precious and fleeting it is, or to become a better person, a more attentive spouse or parent, I will consider my purpose in sharing this story to be fulfilled. I have taken some creative liberties with names and details, and done a bit of paraphrasing, in order to preserve everyone's privacy. I have, at times, drastically simplified the medical jargon to make things more understandable. The few details I have changed are minor and they don't change the story itself.

Prologue

My husband, Harry, and I met in 1976 while we were attending the University of Southern California School of Dentistry. I was earning my Bachelor of Science Degree in Dental Hygiene and Harry was completing his Post-Doctoral Residency in Orthodontics. We married in 1978 and began our life together in Laguna Niguel, California. Laguna Niguel is a lovely family community near the beach with rolling hills, often called "Sea Country." Although it was small back then, it was also growing rapidly, so it was a perfect place to start an orthodontic practice. As Harry's practice grew, I was eventually able to retire from my work as a hygienist, and I fulfilled a lifelong dream of designing and supervising the construction of the house in which we now live. After that, I designed and built Harry's orthodontic office, also in Laguna Niguel.

After enduring several miscarriages, we were blessed with the birth of our son, Harrison, in November of 1994. We had been married for 16 years by then, and had spent that time nurturing friendships within the community and building Harry's practice. We traveled, entertained and remained active with sports and social activities. By the time Harrison came along, we were ready to devote our lives to enjoying as much time with him as we possibly could. When Harrison was ten, Harry retired from his orthodontic practice so that he could spend time coaching baseball, flag football, and golf—the sports that Harrison enjoyed the most. We all relished the idea of being able to spend a great deal of time together in the eight years before Harrison went off to college. To this day, that remains one of the best decisions we ever made. Knowing we could never get those years back, we chose to treasure our time together while Harrison was young and living at home.

In the summer of 2009, Harrison was beginning freshman football practice. We were having a summer of fun social activities and a busy carpooling schedule of summer school, baseball practice, community service, and football practice when suddenly, our "normal life" came to a halt. The night before Harry's "summer adventure" began, we spent the evening with friends at Laguna Beach's Pageant of the Masters. We had a delicious meal together, then sat outside in perfect weather, watching the stunning pageant. By 6:00 the following morning, our lives could not have been more different than they were the night before. Indeed, the calm before the storm....

Thursday, July 23, 2009

A half hour before dawn I awoke to the sound of my husband gasping and thrashing about. My first thought was that he must be having a leg cramp. When I asked him if he was okay, he told me, "No, I'm having bad chest pain." I reached for the phone as I told him I was calling 911. He said he thought that was a good idea. Within minutes, paramedics arrived and diagnosed symptoms of a heart attack.

Our son, Harrison, then fourteen, came into our bedroom as the paramedics were treating Harry and preparing him for a ride to the hospital. Harrison and I followed the ambulance and joined Harry in the ER, where doctors were preparing to catheterize his heart to see if there was an area of blockage. There appeared to be an artery with mild blockage so the decision was made to have a stent placed. Unfortunately, as the stent was being placed, unbeknownst to anyone at the time, it tore the artery. This is extremely rare, but it's one of the possible risks of this procedure. A couple of hours after the placement, Harry began having another episode of severe chest pain and returned to the catheter lab, where the tear in the artery was discovered. A second stent had to be placed to cover the tear and when that one was placed, Harry's iliac and femoral arteries all sustained tears. Once again, this is an extremely rare occurrence. This issue was not immediately evident and several hours later, Harry began experiencing extreme abdominal pain. Blood accumulation from the arterial tears had created painful pressure. Yet another catheterization showed the bleeding and he was in surgery to deal with the tears and bleeding by nine p.m. that evening.

After spending several hours with Harry at the hospital through the morning, Harrison and I went home to feed and walk our dogs and for him to get ready for freshman football practice that afternoon. While we were home, I sent out an email to friends and family, to alert them to what was happening. Little did I know then, I would post an update on his status every day for the next forty-four days. What could have been a very brief visit to the ER turned out to be an ordeal that found Harry hospitalized for forty-four days, with a *zero* percent chance of survival.

This was my first post....

Thursday, July 23, 2009 2:33 p.m.

Hi friends,

I apologize for this impersonal mass email. I'm sure you will find this hard to believe.... Harry had a heart attack this morning. He woke at 5:30 with intense chest pain, I called 911 and the paramedics immediately determined that he was having a heart attack. They whisked him off to the hospital where it was determined that only one of the arteries was mildly occluded, so a stent was placed. Shortly after getting settled in his Cardiac Intensive Care Unit room, the pain returned and he went back to the catheterization room for a second stent placement. He is finally resting comfortably and appears to be out of the woods. We expect that he will be in the ICU until tomorrow and home on Saturday.

Harry is only 59, eats well, exercises a lot, and has no family history of cardiac arrest, so this comes as quite a shock.

This is one of those moments that reminds us how fragile life can be, and that we need to treasure every day with our friends and family members. I hope you will hug your spouses and kids a little tighter tonight.

Thank you to those of you who I have heard from today, for your kind words, your prayers, and your support.

I will keep you posted,
Cathy

In the early afternoon, when we all thought Harry was out of the woods, I took Harrison home to get ready for freshman football practice that afternoon. He went to his room and wrote the following letter to Harry;

"Ahhhh … there's … there's a truck in the … cul-de-sac … maybe it's the trash truck … but wait … what time is it? 5:57 … no that's too early for a trash truck."

"He's at the top of the stairs straight ahead!"

"Alright thank you, ma'am."

Those were the only things that ran through my brain that morning as I ran to the window to see if it really was a nightmare. And it was. Four paramedics in navy blue were walking up the driveway each carrying a bag in which was contents that would help save your life. I grabbed Meeko, who was sitting at the foot of my bed wagging her tail and looking up at the window. I threw on a shirt and said to her, "Let's go see what's wrong, okay?" I don't remember anything that happened until I got to the top of the stairs. The paramedics were streaming into your room, it seemed. I followed closely behind. Mom saw me and I asked her what was wrong.

"Daddy is having some chest pain," she said.

I looked at you, there in bed and my head began to spin. Thoughts ran through my head. Good ones here and there, but predominantly bad thoughts. Thoughts of being the only guy in the house. Thoughts of a eulogy at your funeral. Thoughts of what I would do and what I would become if I didn't have you. Thoughts of pain and suffering. As I looked at your face and heard your groans, I knew how much pain you were in. It tore me apart to see you like that. I wish I could have done something to make it stop right then and there, but I couldn't do a thing. I stood back and watched the paramedics do their thing ... watched them save your life. And soon those thoughts became overwhelming. I had to sit down. I felt the blood draining from my face as it already had from yours. I watched you writhing in pain, and it hurt me, too, to know that you were feeling that. I focused on just you, and it seemed like you were in slow motion and everything else was twice the speed of sound. Like a time lapse on everyone but you and me. I was so close to you, but yet so far away. And as the paramedic said your heart rate was a mere 44 beats per minute, I thought of my heart rate which must have been three times that at the time. Mom then came up to me and told me to go get ready to go to the hospital. As I got dressed I thought of what shirt I could wear to bring me closest to you. I wore my "Maui Dreams Dive Co." shirt. Something we had done and accomplished together. Just you and me. And it brought back memories of Hawaii. Learning to dive with you, diving Molokini with you, diving Turtle Town with you, diving Shark Fin with you, and diving Cathedrals with you and I thought to myself, "This can't be it. We have so much more to do together. So much more diving in so many more places." And as I thought that, some feeling washed over me that told me you would be okay and that told me we would be doing more diving, and not just diving, but more adventures, more trips, more life together. Then I took the girls out back to go potty, and on my way down the stairs, I followed the paramedics, and you in the stretcher. I stood on the first landing and watched you below me with the oxygen mask around your nose and mouth, and for that fleeting moment, I wished I were God. I was above you watching you, and I wished I could just wave my hand and make everything go away, but I couldn't. As you went out the door, I stood and watched and I was able to push out a few words.... "Hang in there, dad!" Then, you were gone, and the race was on to get you to help. I stood there for a moment hoping and praying that you would be ok. I then went to take the girls out. I opened the door and they pranced out like nothing was wrong. I looked at Meeko and I whispered, "Hi, sweetie" and she wagged her tail and looked up at me and I thought maybe she knew. Maybe she knew something was wrong, because the way her eyes looked was not normal. It was concerned and almost sad. Then she turned away and went out on the grass with Boo-Boo. I put all my weight on one leg and cocked my hips as I always do, but this time, the leg with the weight began to shake and tremble, and I held out my hands and they were doing the same. I was scared. I didn't know what to expect. I didn't know if I should be rushing to see you for one last time before you left us, or rushing to be by your side while you recovered. On the way to the hospital, there was one song that ran on a loop it seemed; in my head. It goes like this:

"My old friend, I recall
The times we had hanging on my wall
I wouldn't trade them for gold
Cause they laugh and they cry me

Somehow sanctify me
They're woven in the stories I have told
And tell again

My old friend, I apologize
For the years that have passed
Since the last time you and I
Dusted off those memories
But the running and the races
The people and the places
There's always somewhere else I had to be
And time gets thin, my old friend
Don't know why, don't know why
Don't know why, don't know why

My old friend, this song's for you
Cause a few simple verses
Was the least that I could do
To tell the world that you were here
Cause the love and the laughter
Will live on long after
All of the sadness and the tears
We'll meet again, my old friend ... goodbye,
Goodbye, goodbye, goodbye

My old friend, my old friend
Goodbye, goodbye"
("My Old Friend" Song by Tim McGraw;
Songwriters: Steve Mcewan / Craig Wiseman)

As that rang in my ears, my head spun like the tires on the car. We were driving down the street and I can remember nothing but a fiery red sunrise just over the top of the hospital and I knew that someone up there was with us that morning.

We walked into the hospital and found you in Room 2 at the very back of the hallway. There were more nurses and doctors fluttering around you and one asked how your pain level was now. At home in bed, it was a 7 out of 10. In the ambulance, it increased to an 8, and even morphine didn't touch the pain. Now, sitting in that bed in the hospital, it was a 1, and when you said that word … one … my heart soared like an eagle. I knew we weren't out of the woods quite yet, but there was a very bright light at the end of the tunnel. We wished you luck with the surgery, and 20 minutes later, you were done with it. Mom and I were relieved that everything went well and that you were doing well. The doctor told us that you would be in the CICU in about 20 minutes, so mom and I had breakfast and then came up to see you. When I saw you there, asleep in the bed, I saw that finally, you were pain free. I saw that you were okay. And then as we looked over you, you snored twice, and I knew you were back in business. And when your eyes opened, it was everything I could do not to jump into that hospital bed with you and give you a big old bear hug. And now that you are doing well, I can say that this scared the life out of me. I honestly thought there was a big chance of losing you, and that could not happen. I would feel so empty inside, and so incredibly sad. I would be so sad that crying wouldn't be bad enough. The pain would be too immense to cry. There is no way I could describe how I would feel if you left us … but I don't have to now because you're alright.

What does it mean to me to be a son … your son? It means loving you. It means caring for you in times of need. It means trusting you. It means growing closer and closer to you every second that I am alive. It means seeing you in me. "When I look in the mirror, you're right there in my eyes staring back at me, and I realize: the older I get, the more I can see how much you love my mother and me, and you're doing the best that you can, and I only hope when I have my own family, I hope every day I see a little more of my father in me." ("Song for Dad" Song / Written by Keith Urban) You are an incredible dad, and you could not be replaced by anyone. You are the kind of dad who will lead me to do great things in my life, and I thought some of the stuff I do would have to be in honor of you. Now that you are better,

9

I still want to do things in honor of you, but please don't make me do them in remembrance of you anytime soon! I want my dad to be around when I am a dad myself. I want him to realize the thrill of having grandchildren and being a grandfather. I want him to live his life to the fullest, just like he has been doing. The pain I felt when I saw you in that much pain was unbelievable. I care so much about you, Dad and sometimes, I may not show it, but underneath it all, I do. I really do. I'm always here for you if you need a thing and I'm just glad you are okay. I love you so much and you will forever be in my heart ... even after you move on. Life without you would have been hard, so thank you for staying strong. We need you in our lives, Dad. And I'm so glad you are alright.

I love you Dad, and thank God for all the blessings in our life ... especially this one.

Friday, July 24, 2009 Noon

Dear Friends and Family,

Harry had a rough night last night. His heart is doing okay, but he developed some internal bleeding from the two femoral artery catheterization sites. He was in surgery for several hours last night to repair everything. When I left him at 2:30 this morning, he was still heavily sedated and had a breathing tube in place. His color was decent and his vital signs were good. I know he will make it, but he has been through so much in twenty-four hours—two heart issues and almost five hours of surgery. I have no doubt that he will still be in ICU all day today, and I'm sorry to say we will not be accepting visitors. I'll let you know how he does today and when he will be moved to a regular room and can then accept visitors.

If your well wishes and prayers alone could heal Harry, he would walk out of the hospital today. I cannot even begin to tell you how much we appreciate your overwhelming support.

With great appreciation for your thoughts and prayers,
Harry, Cathy and Harrison

In response to this post and every other that I wrote over the next few months, I received dozens of emails, texts and calls, and on some days hundreds of them. Friends, family, colleagues, patients, acquaintances and even strangers would send me notes of support, prayers, suggestions to take care of myself, and daily offers of help of any kind. With each passing year, during the anniversary days of Harry's hospitalization, I re-read my journal entries and the accompanying responses. The responses never fail to amaze me and it is my pleasure to share many of them with you throughout this book. I was struck repeatedly by the notion that I never knew how so many of our friends felt about Harry and our family. After reading these responses, I have made a concerted effort to tell those that mean the world to us how much I care about them and why I treasure their friendship. I know I am not the only one to have learned this lesson from the summer of 2009. Hundreds of people have told me, over the years, that this was the great benefit of this harrowing experience.

"Adversity introduces a man to himself. Harry will stare down this adversity, fight it toe to toe, and he will conquer it."
~TL

"It's time to now rally the troops, but the troops will be nothing but POSITIVE!! I am contacting everyone I know that is extremely faithful, across the country, to storm Heaven with prayers. We need one hundred percent positive energy to permeate the hospital and beyond.... Believing and knowing that Harry will pull through and give us years of teasing about how he scared us all so much!"
~MF

"Oh, my goodness, Cathy! I am in shock. When I saw Harry's name in the subject line, my first thought was that he was being recognized for something he did to enrich the lives of others. I'm stunned and so very sorry."
~JH

"I am so very sad to hear this news! I am in SHOCK. I have just returned from a day with my daughter and grandchildren, a day so full of life and promise. Your email throws me back to reality and does, indeed, remind me of how fragile life is. My prayers are with all three of you and our thoughts will be with you constantly. Thank you for keeping us informed."
~MB

"What????? No, no, no. I am teary-eyed just reading these emails. I love, respect, and admire Harry so much.... WOW. Beneath his charming smile and mischievous grin is a tough as nails achiever and fighter. You don't accomplish so much like he has without a will to win, a will to fight, a will to live. If anyone survives this crisis, surely it will be Harry. So believe in his burning drive to return to the wonderful life you and he and Harrison enjoy, a life I know he loves and cherishes so much. Sending lots of positive mojo to my good buddy."
~SS

Friday, July 24, 2009 11:48 p.m.

I'm happy to say that Harry seems to be doing better now, but it was a tough day for him. Less than 10 hours after his lengthy surgery that ended at 1:30 this morning, a clot broke off the femoral artery catheterization site and traveled down his right leg. Blood flow was blocked and Harry's right foot had no pulse. A quick decision needed to be made on how to handle the clotting. Anti-clotting medication is a life-threatening risk so soon after vascular surgery. But, if blood flow to the foot continued to be constricted, Harry would have had to eventually have his foot amputated, and the doctors weren't sure if Harry could have survived the serious amputation surgery. The attending cardiologist told me that Harry is the most seriously ill patient in the Intensive Care Unit right now.

The decision was made to administer the anti-clotting medication. Around seven tonight, a thready pulse was felt in Harry's right foot, and there was no evidence of bleeding anywhere else. By the time Harrison and I left the hospital tonight at 8:45, there was a steady, healthy pulse in both feet, and no bleeding anywhere else. Harry is still heavily sedated, but slowly shook his head yes when we told him that we can't wait to bring him home. Harry will be in ICU again tomorrow, and cannot have visitors. We are hoping that tomorrow brings no more complications!

THANK YOU FOR YOUR SUPPORT!

We are humbled by the outpouring of love, kindness and prayers from you....

The Whites

The decision of whether to choose blood thinners or possible eventual amputation was left up to me. I sat alone in Harry's room and looked at his unconscious body, picked up his hand and said, "What the heck has happened to us, to our normal lives? Forty-eight hours ago, life was wonderful and now, here we are in this hideous nightmare." It was the thought of our "normal life" that made me choose the blood thinner. I trusted in Harry's strength and overall health and I knew he would be devastated, to say the least, to wake up to an amputation. Blood thinners were administered and it turned out to be the right decision. Little did I know, this was the first of many difficult decisions I would need to make on Harry's behalf over the next month and a half.

Saturday, July 25, 2009 4:27 p.m.

So far, so good ...

So far, so good. Harry had an angiogram this morning to check the clots in his right foot. His situation is better, but there are still a few clots left, so he will continue blood thinning medication for at least another twelve hours. He is still heavily sedated, as the doctors don't want him disrupting another clot from the femoral artery locations. It's now thirty-eight hours since the completion of the vascular abdominal surgery, and with each passing hour, the threat of bleeding in those areas becomes less and less.

Harry's brother, Bill, who is an emergency room physician, flew in from Colorado early yesterday, Friday morning, to be with us. He has been a great source of help, accurate information and support.

The last time Harry was able to communicate with us was 4 p.m. on Thursday. He rarely opens his eyes, and even then, does not focus on us. He is still on a respirator, so he couldn't talk if he awakened anyway. This is a good thing, though, because he needs to rest and to heal. He needs to stay still, so that he doesn't test the staff with yet another complication! We are hopeful that he will be out of CICU on Monday or Tuesday.

I cannot thank you enough for all of your emails and phone calls, and I can't wait to share with Harry your overwhelming words of support and love. I'd like to think that we didn't need any reminders to live each day to the fullest. I thought we were already doing that. However, the lesson is there for all of us. Please learn from our challenges this week—please take the time to tell your friends and family how much you care about them. Please honor Harry by making a commitment to live each day to the fullest, with grace, forgiveness and love.
Cathy

Some of my favorite emails and texts were the funny ones that helped to ease the tension of these difficult days.

"When Harry awakens, would you please tell him that any thought I had on retirement and its wonders has vanished. If this is what retirement gets ya, I'm working forever."
~PC

"I'm very hurt that Harry is so sick ... he is my counselor, my buddy, my life coach! I can see his smiling face in my mind's eye from two thousand miles away. Next time he wakes up, please remind him that not only is September 9th your 31st wedding anniversary, it's also National Breast Appreciation Day! ;-)
My love to you three,"
~Bill S

"He did this to get out of making more of those darn mouthguard impressions, didn't he?"
~RM

"Thank you for sending this update. We are also concerned for Harry and for you and H. I was planning to make a quick visit today, but I'm sure there are so many people that care about him, the hospital has run out of parking by now. Please let him know that we, just like everyone else, are thinking of him and love him."
~JH

"I am coming to the hospital in a speedo to do a little dance for Harry as he recovers.... Hopefully bringing a tear to his eye. We read your missive glued to the screen and sending thoughts, wishes and prayers to your family. Remind Harry, should he stay too long in that hospital bed, the odds of me actually showing up dancing in a speedo will increase."
~SM

Sunday, July 26, 2009 10:46 a.m.

A Hopeful Day ...

Harry had a comfortable night. Yesterday, his nurse changed his sedation medication, as he was very agitated every time he began to wake up. Since the change, he has done much better—he is calmer, more stable. He looks better, too!

Harry was weaned off of the blood thinners through the night, and went in this morning at 10:00 for the angiogram to check the right foot. It looks and feels so good right now—it's pink and warm—very different from the blue/cold of two days ago. But, his hematocrit and need for frequent blood transfusions suggest that he is bleeding somewhere else (hopefully, it is only 'seepage'), so the vascular surgeon said he absolutely had to get off the blood thinner. Later today, doctors hope to get him off the ventilator so that he can breathe on his own and begin to eat and recover. He will probably be in CICU through Tuesday.

I'll let you know the results of the angiogram and how Harry does through the afternoon. We think that he will be a different man by this time tomorrow!

Yesterday, I read Harry some of your emails, and he fluttered his eyes briefly several times while I was talking to him. He feels your love and support. He is anxious to come back to us, and I am anxious to share with him how much he is loved by you....
Cathy

Our friend, Jeff, had recently gone through a life-threatening liver transplant. I love this man fiercely and he is the purest example of friendship and brotherhood. Whenever he would send me messages during this entire ordeal, they meant EVERYTHING to me. He knew the graveness of Harry's situation and was able to share with me his own experiences and those of his family. Hearing from Jeff always made me feel that I wasn't going through this alone and he continually gave me hope that Harry would survive. This is the first of the many helpful messages that he sent me over the next two months:

"I am in total shock, as I know you are. Hare Dog is my idol and god when it comes to health and happiness. My

thoughts and prayers go without saying. I'm crying as I type this, but I know how strong he is and how much he loves his family; so at this point we all take a deep breath and let time work its magic and heal his body.

I get the shakes each time I enter a hospital, but for Hare Dog, I'm happy to set up camp in the lobby and supply food to friends and family!

Cath, you are the best of the BEST in keeping everyone informed and helping to relieve the tremendous concern that we all have. Hopefully, it has helped you, too. You have always tried to be superwoman, but with something of this magnitude you must take a deep breath, clear your head, and try to relax, even if it's just for a few moments. You are Hare Dog's life support system and just as important as any piece of equipment in his room. Trust me on this—he may not be able to communicate as well as he would like and many times his mind will be getting it, but his body will be too medicated and too exhausted to respond. He will not remember a lot of the things that you are saying or doing for him, but the "feelings" get through. I can remember having my feet rubbed, my hair stroked, and nice, encouraging words being said, but I was too tired to open my eyes and my body was not responding to what my mind was telling it to do.

It's going to be okay—Hare Dog is very strong and his will is going to prevail.

To be honest this is the first thing I've seen that somewhat proves he isn't perfect! I swear, until this happened, I thought he was not human! This is going to be a great life lesson for your son, I know it was for my son and believe it or not we are all better human beings because of what happened.

Chin up, big smile, words of encouragement, and once that trach is out, you will see a big Hare Dog grin. Not a full smile, he'll keep that for later, but a little s#$@-eatin' grin like 'See—I can pull out of anything!'

Get some sleep.... It's not over but he will be heading home soon.

We love you, Cath,"
J, J and P

Sunday, July 26, 2009 9:52 p.m.

Thank God! Harry is Doing Better Tonight!

The angiogram this morning showed no more clots and the foot circulation is normal. Blood thinning medication stopped at 9 a.m., but Harry still needs to be kept sedated until the threat of more bleeding has passed. Tomorrow morning, his sedation will be gradually decreased and he will be tested to make sure he can breathe on his own (which he hasn't done since Thursday evening). Then, the ventilator will be removed, and normal recovery can begin.

Today, Harry looked like he was sleeping, whereas the last couple of days, he looked heavily sedated. He is responding better to things we say to him. Occasionally, his eyes flutter open and his fingers weakly respond to our hands. Tonight, I asked him if he was trying to let everyone know that he is okay, and he slowly nodded yes!

I have read every one of your emails, listened to every message, read every text. If I haven't responded personally to you yet, I will eventually, because I want each of you to know how much I appreciate what you have said. Your words of encouragement and support, your offers of help, your prayers, your humor ... have all helped me get through these past few days with hope and optimism. Harry knows he has so much to live for—a community of friends and family that love and appreciate what a remarkable man he is. I know he feels it and is fighting to be back with us.

Good-night!
Cathy

"One of the most common phrases currently spoken in our household is, "How's Harry?" I had the recent pleasure of going on the 8th grade DC trip, in which Harry was also a parent/chaperone. We were on different buses, but every time we crossed paths it was just like every other time I've ever been around Harry. An authentic interest in everything going on with our family, followed by compliments,

19

congratulations and words of positive encouragement. It was on this trip, after stepping back up onto Bus 1, that I had the fleeting thought: "Harry always makes people feel good. Quite a gift." This truth is even more significant to me now. Like the many, many others, we pray for Harry. Anytime I wake up in the middle of the night, I talk to Him. Hey, I figure we're both flat on our back with nothing else going on so perhaps there's an open line of communication there. We all know God is present here. I pray for a full, quick, and miraculous recovery for my friend, Harry White.
God bless,"
~SO

"I was frantically checking my emails, waiting for an update. I can't tell you how flooded with relief I am that the big guy is doing better. Situations like yours make me take a look at life and really appreciate how great things are. We are so fortunate! Please let Harrison know that we are thinking of him. These are trying times for anyone, but for a son ... oh my. Stay strong, get some rest and rejoice in Harry's healing."
~CD

"Boy, the events of these past few days have really hit me. It makes me think more clearly about what is really important. I'm so sorry that you have had to endure this unfortunate week, but there are many positives as we ponder our lives and how precious the small things are. I have hugged my husband, children, parents, siblings and friends just a little harder and a little longer since hearing about Harry. When he is up and around and smiling like usual, I'm going to thank him for opening my heart even bigger than I thought it already was. Please let us know if we can help you in any way."
~BH

Monday, July 27, 2009 11:06 p.m.

Still Doing Okay …

Harry is still doing well tonight, but has not yet come off the ventilator. This isn't a set-back or complication, but getting him off of it is taking a little longer than expected. After spending four days in heavy sedation on three different drugs, the cut-back needs to be slow, or Harry will go through painful, uncomfortable withdrawals. He experienced some of that today. At the same time that the staff is cutting back on sedation, they are gradually decreasing the need for the ventilator, and Harry is beginning to take some breaths on his own. We now expect that the ventilator will come out tomorrow. The progress is slower than we had hoped, but at least it is going in the right direction! Maybe ICU until Thursday now—

In his more relaxed moments, Harry still responds to us by small nods. This morning, he actually tried to smile a couple of times, which isn't easy, given that his mouth is taped around a breathing tube! His eyes have fluttered open more today, and the focus looks better.

Harry had a CT scan late this afternoon to check the status of his internal organs and the report was that there is no new abdominal bleeding. We will have more comprehensive results tomorrow, but are expecting that all is well.

Harry's daytime ICU nurse (Sheila) for the past three days has been phenomenal. Tomorrow is her day off, but she switched work days with another nurse so that she can continue to care for Harry. She said that he has an aura about him, that she knows he is someone for whom God wants her to give special care. She doesn't want to take a day off until she sees Harry smile at his family and is able to give us hugs.

I spoke to the cardiologist at length today and among many other things, he expressed that he thinks Harry is a very strong man and an extremely lucky one. He said he must have a strong will to live. When I asked him if he thought Harry was finally out of the woods, he said,

"Yes, I believe he now is."

Cathy

"Harry's nurse is right.... There are some people who just stand out in life and Harry is one of them! That smile, that warm greeting he always gives, his kind and considerate ways. The close connection he has with Harrison and so many of the other kids at our school has always been wonderful to watch through the years. He certainly seems to have his priorities straight. When he comes completely out of sedation, I think Sheila will realize how very astute she really is!"
~LF

"Okay, now I know it's HARRY—five plus days in CICU under heavy sedation and still his charisma won't stop. As for the doctor saying Harry has a strong will to live—I am certain that when he is able to speak to you, he will tell you that even though he was on all those meds, he was still in there. He was listening and loving and fighting from the inside to get back to you and H and all of the great times you have ahead of you."
~JH

"We continue to lift up Harry in our prayers every day. I must tell you I have always thought nurses are very special people, if not angels. One year in my Bible study fellowship discussion group, half of the ladies were nurses ... and many of them were critical care nurses. I always felt comforted knowing how many of them were studying God's word and then applying it to their work. What a blessing for Harry to be in Sheila's hands.... Not by chance, I'm sure."
~TW

"The major factor in all of this is HW himself. When the chips are down, Harry is a fighter. His ever-present optimistic outlook and his faith in himself, his family and community have and will serve him well. I would wish his circumstances on no one, but if I had to bet on anyone to beat this thing, it would be HW. You are all in our hourly thoughts and we anxiously await word that everything is going to be A-okay."
~RL

"There is renewed peace in the air tonight. Anyone who knows Harry cannot help but be a little stunned by the fragility and preciousness of life. Like countless others, I have never known anyone more alive than Harry. Frankly, I think God may have entertained the idea of bringing him to Heaven, but then quickly realized that there was not a big enough yard for this force of life to play.... If I can do anything to make the next days and weeks easier or better, please do not hesitate to ask. Your family is in my constant thoughts and prayers. I love you guys sooooo much and I am standing guard."
~ME

"Thank you for staying so strong and positive! We all need that. Our thoughts and prayers are with the three of you each moment of every day. Harry's nurse is right.... There is something very special about him. I could tell that from the first moment we met. He loves life and is blessed by God. It shows in his happiness, friendliness and willingness to go out of his way for other people."
~NM

Tuesday, July 28, 2009 9:27 p.m.

Slowly, but Surely ... We are Progressing!

Harry is doing well.... He is resting comfortably, but is mildly sedated. The respirator is still in and will be until his body slowly adjusts to the weaning of sedation and the resumption of breathing. His body is working diligently to rid itself of many, many fluids introduced over the last few days. Yesterday, his hands and feet looked a bit like the Michelin Man. Today, I can actually feel ridges of bone beneath the skin. His kidneys excreted 3 liters of fluid today—no complications *there*!

Harry's CT scan from late yesterday showed no problems with bleeding. His eyes focused better today than any time since Thursday. He did a little bit of nodding, and would slowly turn his head toward my cheek when I talked to him and kissed him on his cheek. A couple of days ago, there were thirteen bags hanging on his IV post. Today, there were only five. We are making progress!

When I left tonight, "Angel Sheila" was just finishing her shift. We are so lucky—she will be back again tomorrow to care for Harry! Then, bless her heart, she has four days off. She deserves it! Today, while Harrison was at school doing community service and football practice, I was able to spend several hours alone with Harry, and to observe what an incredible job Sheila is doing for us. She never stops! She's calm and loving, and so diligent. She is one very special woman. We will never forget what she has done for us.

Your emails, phone messages, and texts renew my strength every day. Harrison and I are doing well, but I know that would not be so without your support. Your loving thoughts, cute stories, offers of help, and fervent prayers are bringing us through this.

Cathy

"For everyone in my family, the first thing we think of in the morning is, "How is Harry?" We rush to our email and always take a deep breath before reading your next post. We are so

happy to hear that he is doing better. I'll bet God hasn't heard so many prayers for the recovery and strength of one person in many, many years! The Stanford Cardinal fight and of course with all the teams he has coached for the Tartans, a big Tartan fight is in there too! My prayers to the Lord are with you three for continued strength and healing."
~LF

"You are all continuously in my prayers. Harry is an amazing man and his time here is not finished. He has much more life to live. He contributes so much to everyone's life that he touches and I know he will continue to do so for many, many more years to come. He is fighting strongly to come back to you and H. Please, please, please let me help you in any way that I can."
~SF

"Your nurse, Angel Sheila, obviously went into this field to be in this moment. Isn't it interesting that the little things are such huge gifts in life? You recognize them, as do I and we will thank God for all of those."
~JM

"On several occasions, we have passed Dr. White in our community and we always enjoy seeing him. We have always admired him for his quick smile and warm wave. His friendliness often comes as a surprise to us, but always leaves a lasting impression and puts a smile on our faces as we see each other on the road. I wish I had already shared this with him, but every day we try to be more like him and mimic that quick neighborly smile and warm wave as we pass other residents and friends in our community. Dr. White's friendliness is something truly unique and we will continue to follow his lead in that regard."
~DT

"Here is my prayer for tonight.... Lord, you know this man who lays before you in this bed. We are pleased and proud

25

with your work on him, to heal this very important man. Every one of your children is important to you, but I believe Harry is extra special and that you are extra fond of him. Some people are important to mortals because of their fame and fortune, but Harry is important to YOU because he makes everyone around him feel that they are most important. That is such a rare quality and I ask you to spare his life and let him return to us."
~JD

Batzi is one of my dearest friends ... a sister of choice to me, Harrison's second mom and my next-door neighbor. She was often with me at the hospital and was one of the greatest members of my support system. She drove Harrison to and from football practice, cooked for us, walked our dogs, graciously greeted friends and family members at the hospital, a little bit of everything. She was standing with me this Tuesday afternoon when someone walked up and asked me some questions about Harry. My answer was diplomatically positive and a bit incomplete. After this friend walked away, Batzi said she noticed that I didn't really give the full answer. I told her that I just couldn't. For the past week (and for much longer as it would turn out), I felt like a cog in the center of a wheel. In every direction that I looked, there was someone who relied on me to be positive, upbeat and hopeful. In one direction was Harry, another direction was Harrison. There were Harry's 92 and 85-year-old parents, the doctors and nurses, friends and other family members all looking to me for hope. I didn't want that veneer of positivity to crack because I thought that if I began to show some of the fear I was experiencing, others would, too, and the aura would shift. Yes, I did sugarcoat that conversation and it would be the first of many, but I felt it was very necessary. I especially didn't want Harrison to be any more afraid than he already was, so I was careful with my own behavior and words in front of him and in front of anyone who might repeat stories in front of him. It was difficult, and the need to show more confidence than I felt lasted for another month. It was tough to keep things in, but in retrospect, I would do it all again this same way.

Wednesday, July 29, 2009 9:13 p.m.

The Ventilator is Out!

The ventilator came out around 1 p.m. today. Harry is breathing well on his own. His heart is doing *great*—since the placement of the stents, his heart has been very strong and stable. The circulation in his feet is perfect now, and swelling is diminishing by the hour. But, since the weaning of the three sedative drugs, Harry has been fairly agitated. This is not unexpected after spending six days under heavy sedation.

We expect that Harry will be in ICU until Friday, in a cardiac telemetry room for at least two more days, and a regular room for two days after that.

Harry's throat and vocal cords are swollen and irritated, so his nurse, "Angel Sheila," didn't want him talking today. No matter how much we told him not to talk, he kept trying. He's still pretty out of it, too—not opening his eyes much, not responding easily to questions or requests. It's very hard to understand him right now, but I finally figured out that his first question was, "Where am I?" After that, he said, "Hot" and sure enough, he was perspiring. Next came, "Cat, Cat, Cat," which is his nickname for me. Then he said, "I wanna get up." When Sheila told him that he couldn't get out of bed because he was sick, he said, "I'm fine, I'm fine." (that one cracked me up—it is *so* Harry!) And, lastly, my personal favorite....

"Cat, let's go home. I want to go home. I want to go home."

Until tomorrow,
Cathy and the H-Men

"Of course telling Harry not to talk wouldn't work. If you are a talker, like we are, and you haven't talked in almost a week, your word count is way behind! He has several thousand words to make up for!! We are still praying hard for a speedy and full recovery Harry has an amazing heart and it will heal one hundred percent."
~SB

*"Here is my 'this guy is amazing story' about Harry....
I had just found out that I was going to have twin boys and
needless to say, I was in a state of shock and not quite at
the point of 'pure joy.' More at a point of 'Oh, man, what am
I going to do?' Of course, I am at a much better point of
happiness now, but the shock of dealing with two little guys
at the same time scared me a bit. Everyone kept saying
'God knows you can handle it or he wouldn't have given you
two blessings.' I kept saying to myself, 'I sure hope so!' Then
literally right in the midst of my fear, I sat in the bleachers
at one of our middle school sports awards banquets, was
watching Harry interact with Harrison, and it all changed
for me. I thought to myself, 'That's what I will have and
it will be double!' I saw Harry hug and kiss Harrison and
what was extra special is that Harrison appreciated the love
(unlike many middle school boys do at that age). That was
my inspiration—to parent my boys like you and Harry have
parented Harrison. The relationship Harry and Harrison have
is just like the relationship my dad and I have. My goal is to be
a dad like that!"*
~MA

*"I just learned this morning about what's going on with Harry
and I am stunned. I thought it couldn't be Harry White!!!
There is no one that will fight harder than Harry, knowing
how much he loves you and Harrison. He is an incredible and
strong person who loves life and it will be a short time before
he is out of the hospital living life as only he can do. I know
you have heard this a million times, but I would be so honored
if we could help you in any way."*
~JG

*"Woo hoo! I especially like the 'I'm fine ... I want to go
home!' Well, if he just had a pair of red, sparkly shoes maybe
you could get him home. We will nickname him 'Harry D' for
Dorothy—I want to go home—White! Feisty is good, good,
good—keep the great news coming!"*
~JM

"Oh man. I just learned of Harry's ordeal. Dear God … My prayers and thoughts are with all of you. I love this guy and he will pull through. Please remind him that this heart stuff is a little extreme to get out of doing the dishes."
~PJ

Another poignant message from Jeff, the liver transplant recipient:
"How fantastic! It is so fabulous that you've been keeping track of all this and have it written down. At some point in the not so near future, it will really be a treat to relive these moments thanks to your tenacity. I assure you, Harry will not remember any of this without being reminded and then only certain moments might come back. I am sure you have done it, but I really enjoyed having just a couple pictures of P and J where I could see them. When no one else was in the room, I would just stare at them and think about all that we would do when I got out. Please, please tell everyone to stay at home except family for the first couple of weeks when Hare Dog gets home. It is so exhausting to have to entertain friends, even for a short while. People try to do what they think is best by coming by and unless they are told point-blank, a guy like Hare Dog will have twenty people a day stopping by and recovery will take much longer. I can't wait to see him but I will wait until he's ready to see me. Tell him to escape before they try to get him to like chicken prepared two thousand different ways. The only dish I didn't see was chicken ice cream! How good does Hawaii sound about now? If you want somebody to sit around and go for short walks on the beach, we are available. Okay, enough—sleep well, all is good, time will heal and I'll make you the same promise that I made to my wife when I woke up; the second half of our life is going to be even better than the first. It will be for you guys, too. Give him a big, wet, sloppy kiss and then tell him it was from me— watch for the s#$@-eatin' grin!"
~Jeff

Thursday, July 30, 2009 11:11 p.m.

Ugh ... A Setback

I was just writing this update when the phone rang—not a good thing at 10:50 p.m. Harry has had to be re-intubated, because he began running a fever, and his blood pressure was not detectable. Not sure if it is an infection or bleeding. When we left him around 8:00 p.m., he was doing pretty well—wanting to eat, wanting to get out of bed, wanting to "go down to the car." Poor Harry—he's been through so much already....

He needs your prayers!
Cathy

Friday, July 31, 2009 9:35 a.m.

God Saved Harry this Morning

Last night, after hearing from the nurse that Harry had taken a turn for the worse, I told Harrison that I was just going to sit with Daddy for an hour or two. When I got to the hospital, I was shocked at how bad he looked.

After a while the doctor told me it would be better for me if I weren't in the room, so I went to the waiting room. About 1:30 a.m., I heard the announcement:

"Code Blue, CICU, Bed 4 ... Code Blue, CICU, Bed 4 ... "

I was painfully aware that it was ... *Harry's bed*....

Twenty minutes later a nurse came to get me and said, "Mrs. White, we've been giving your husband CPR for twenty minutes now, and I'm sorry, but it doesn't look good. We are taking him in for emergency surgery, but his chances are not good. I think you should come with me now, so that you can see him alive for the last time and to say good-bye."

So I did just that. I accompanied the gurney downstairs to the OR, keeping my eyes on the big, strong angel in blue scrubs who was straddling Harry's body, keeping his heart going. Everyone around me kept assuring me that they would do everything humanly possible to save Harry's life.

I called Harry's parents and brothers, and called my parents and brother. My mom was already at our house with Harrison. The rest of us all huddled around watching the clock. After a half hour, a nurse came out and said, "We have a pulse!" Another hour after that, the nurse came back and said that Harry was holding his own, that the surgeon had found and stopped the bleeding, and was checking to make sure that he had gotten it all. Another hour later, the surgeon came out to speak with us. He said that Harry is in extremely critical condition, and that it will be touch and go for at least three days. He cannot close up the incision yet, because Harry's organs are so swollen from the trauma of the bleeding and CPR compressions. He will need many subsequent surgeries to complete the closing of his abdomen. Right now, Harry looks ... *awful*. I am never queasy, but when I saw him two hours after surgery, I almost passed out. He was unrecognizable because of all of the swelling and bruising on his face. Even Harry's brother, Bill, an ER doctor, was shocked and shaken at Harry's appearance. Bill and I wouldn't let Harry's parents see him ... because he looked so bad.

When he finished speaking with us, the surgeon had tears in his eyes. He hugged me and said, "God saved your husband tonight."

I can't begin to describe how I feel right now. Of course, I am frightened beyond description. And, seeing what Harry's poor body has gone through breaks my heart so badly—it's impossible for me to stop thinking about what that battered body means and what he has endured. The thought of having to tell Harrison that his father died tonight ... the worst feeling I've ever had.

Keep the prayers coming. Harry's road to recovery will now be very long and extremely difficult. I know he will make it. He is strong and healthy, and we know he "wants to go home," but, he needs all the prayers we can say for him.
Cat

There is much to be shared about this evening.

Every day since the surgery that Harry had the first night he was in the hospital, a week prior, his vascular surgeon would tell me that he was concerned about a large hematoma that had formed in Harry's abdomen as a result of the iliac and femoral bleed. He was concerned about the hematoma rupturing and mentioned that to me every day. It was one of the things that I kept to myself.

On the evening of Thursday, July 30, around 10:45, I tucked Harrison into bed. For the entire forty-four days that Harry was in the hospital, Harrison slept in my room on Harry's side of the bed. The morning that the paramedics took Harry to the hospital, they took his T-shirt off and used it to wipe the sweat from his chest before they put the monitors on him. When we found the shirt crumpled on the floor that first evening, Harrison picked it up and smelled it and said it smelled like Dad. So, I folded it and put it on the bedside table and it remained there for Harrison to smell every night before sleep until Harry finally came home.

After kissing Harrison good night, I turned off the light, closed the door and went down the hall to my office to post the update for the day.

I had just written a line or two when the phone rang. My eyes snapped to the clock above my desk and when I saw it was 10:50, my stomach sank and my heart began racing. Harry's nurse told me that he had taken a turn for the worse, that he had developed a fever and his blood pressure was *undetectable!* The nurse's voice was very somber as he explained that it could either be from bleeding or from fever, but he wanted to stress to me that the situation had become much more serious. I told him I was on my way. Instinct told me that the hematoma had ruptured and that the lack of detectable BP was from internal bleeding. Harrison had heard the phone as well and was not asleep yet. I went to my room and … I had to lie to him…. I told him that the nurse said Dad was very uncomfortable and that I was just going to go sit with him for a little bit to hold his hand and try to calm him down. I told him that if I couldn't be back within the hour, I would call my parents to come stay with him.

Upon arrival at Harry's room, I knew he was in serious danger of losing his life. As bad as some of the moments had been up to now, this was completely different and very precarious. There were about eight staff members in the room, each working diligently, with quiet focus. The intensivist, who was the quarterback of the team, told me that they were all doing everything they could. He said he suspected that Harry had massive internal bleeding and that there was so much blood filling his abdomen, it was making his blood pressure undetectable because not enough of it was circulating through his blood vessels. Harry's abdomen was so distended, he like looked he was seven months pregnant. His coloring was truly white as a sheet and he had been re-intubated. The respirator was making Harry's body jerk and jump, which only added to the ugliness of an already unreal scene. After about ten minutes, the doctor said he thought it would be better if I waited in the waiting room. Looking back, I am certain that he suspected that Harry's heart was going to stop and he didn't want me in the room to witness that.

When I arrived in the quiet, empty, softly-lit waiting room, I called my parents and told them that Harry had taken a turn for the worse and I was back at the hospital with him. I explained that Harrison was by himself and asked if they would please go to him, which they said they would do immediately.

The minutes in that silent room seemed to pass so slowly. It felt like I had been standing there waiting for news for hours, but it was probably only about twenty minutes, when I heard "Code Blue" called for Harry's bed … "CICU Bed 4" … I watched, with my heart pounding, as a team of doctors and nurses ran down the hall with the crash cart. The doors of the CICU swallowed them up and again it was eerily silent. Five minutes later, my phone rang and I saw that it was Harrison. It was everything I could do to calm my voice and answer the phone. He asked me how Harry was doing and of course I lied again to him, telling him that Daddy was going to be okay, but that he was still uncomfortable. I told him that I was going to stay there longer and that my parents were on their way to stay with him. They lived about a half hour away and I had called them twenty-five minutes before. I hoped to God that I was able to keep the fear out of my voice and he said, "Give Dad a big kiss for me, okay?"

I felt like I had been waiting again for hours to find out what was happening to Harry. But after about twenty minutes, a nurse came to get me and motioned for me to follow her into the Grieving Room, a small room adjacent to the main ICU waiting room. We didn't sit. She turned to me and the look on her face scared me so badly I could barely breathe. She said, "I know you heard the Code Blue call. We've been giving CPR to your husband for twenty minutes and it doesn't look good. We are doing everything we can but you should come with me now in case it's the last time you see him alive. He's still unconscious, but you might want to tell him goodbye."

I'm not sure where I gained the strength to walk down the hall. Years later, I can still so vividly see that room—it was like a stage— Harry on the gurney, every person in the room focused on their jobs. Doctors and nurses were taking turns giving Harry CPR. The nurse who accompanied me told me that the vascular surgeon and trauma surgeon had been called to the hospital and as soon as the Operating Room was ready, they would take Harry downstairs for surgery. Everyone in the room kept reassuring me that they were doing everything that they could. About five minutes later the phone rang, a nurse picked it up and when she put it down, she yelled, "They're ready, let's move." Already drenched in sweat from his efforts, a large, athletic male nurse jumped on the gurney and straddled Harry's body. He continued CPR on the way out of CICU, down the elevator, and into the OR.

The nurse who was with me told me that I needed to call someone to be with me. I called Harry's parents, my dad, and Bill and Kathi, who were in a hotel nearby. I'm not sure how I made that phone call to Harry's parents—waking them in the middle of the night to tell them to come to the hospital, because it looked like their son was about to die.

At this hour in the middle of the night, the front door to the hospital was locked and the only entry was through the emergency room door. I had mentioned that to everyone who I called and told them that I would meet them at the emergency room door to take them back to the OR waiting room.

I was walking through a dim hallway on my way to the ER when suddenly the most intense feeling of physical and emotional euphoria passed through me, making every hair on my body stand on end. I stopped and slowly looked around me as if searching for something that had passed by. The hallway was dim and empty. The feeling passed and I continued to the ER door to wait. I felt momentarily guilty for having such an immensely joyous moment and I was a bit spooked by the intense feeling.

Harry and I are certain that he died that night and came back to life. As he began to recover, he told me stories of some out-of-body experiences he had and I will share those later in the book. As for this night and that sudden, overwhelming sense of euphoria, I believe that is when Harry's soul came back to us. It was several months later when Harry was describing being above his body and looking down at everybody in the blue scrubs and I realized that it wasn't in the CICU room (where everyone was wearing different colors) that he had died and returned (as I had once believed) … it was in the Operating Room. The OR is where everyone was in blue scrubs and as soon as he said *everyone* was in blue, I knew it had to be in the OR. That's when it hit me. That is where Harry was when those feelings passed through me. I believe with all my heart that my moment of euphoria was because that was when Harry came back to us.

Harry's parents arrived first, then my dad, then Bill and Kathi. We all gathered in the waiting room of the OR and once again the minutes seemed to drag like days. I told them what had happened, about the late phone call from the nurse, calling my parents to go to our house to be with Harrison, seeing Harry in the room when I arrived, the Code Blue call, the CPR on the way to surgery. We were all grateful that he had

35

made it to this point but none of us would have been surprised to hear if he did not make it through the night. There were many tears shed as we each sat in our private hells of fear.

I was seated in a chair facing the door and had just looked at my watch for the thousandth time. The door to the room burst open and the nurse looked straight at me, gave a little half-smile and said, "We have a heartbeat!" She told us it would still be another hour or two before the surgery was complete and that when it was, the surgeon would come to talk to us. She warned us that Harry was still in extremely critical condition but that for now, he was alive! She returned about an hour later and informed us that Harry was still alive and that he was holding his own.

When the exhausted surgeon walked into the room an hour or so later, I stood up and slowly walked towards him looking intently at his face for signs of whether the news was good or bad. He whispered, "He's still alive." He ran his hands through his sweaty hair and hugged me, gulping with the effort not to cry. He then sat with us and gave us all the details. Harry's internal bleeding was so severe that when the abdomen had filled with blood, the heart had no room to expand and no blood to pump. As soon as much of the blood was removed from the abdomen, they were able to get his heart beating again. He received twenty-six units of blood transfusion that night. The doctor said he suspected that this all happened because the hematoma ruptured, just as he had feared it might.

He also explained that the eighteen-inch incision, from his sternum to his pelvis, needed to remove the blood from his abdomen, could not be closed at this time. The internal bleeding and 45 minutes of CPR traumatized the internal organs so severely that the swelling of all the organs eliminated the possibility of closure. Gore-Tex had been put in place to protect the abdominal organs and it was the surgeon's hope that over the next several days the swelling would reduce enough to allow closing of the incision. He also explained that when the pressure of the abdomen is not what the body expects and wants it to be, the organs can shut down. He warned us that this could lead to Abdominal Compartment Syndrome, which has close to a *zero* percent chance of survival. Harry was alive, but he was in extremely critical condition.

When the surgeon stood up to leave, he again hugged me and said,

"God saved your husband tonight. There is no other explanation for why he survived this night."

I have no doubt that the hand of God was at work that night, but I know, too, that every staff member in the ICU room and operating room worked tirelessly to save Harry. From Harry's night nurse, who recognized that his condition was worsening, to the intensivist who came back to ICU as he was about to leave for the evening, to every nurse and surgeon ... I am certain their dedication to doing everything humanly possible, to go above and beyond to save Harry contributed to his miraculous survival that evening.

About an hour after we finished talking with the surgeon, Harry was moved back to a room in CICU. Bill, his parents and I went upstairs to see him. Bill and I walked into the room first and stopped in our tracks. Harry's face was so swollen, he was unrecognizable. Bill and I both said at the same time, "Mom and Dad CANNOT see him like this!" and Bill quickly left the room to catch them in the hall before they saw Harry. Both of Harry's eyes were swollen shut, his face was beet red and his lips were cut and swollen to the size of a fat finger. He looked like the loser in a prize fight. He smelled like blood ... and death. The nurses had done their best to clean him up but there were still wisps of wiped blood on his forehead, neck and arms. I stood there looking at him, wondering how a human being could survive what he had been through.

Bill and I gaped at Harry, at his battered face and body, shaking our heads at one another and at this unbelievable nightmare that had transpired over the last six hours. With assurances from the nurses that they would call me if there were any changes, Bill and I joined his parents, my dad, and Kathi in the CICU waiting room. One by one, everyone else drifted off to sleep. I wanted to as well, but sleep never came. In a haze of fatigue, I watched the sun come up, thinking constantly about the fact that we weren't close to being out of the woods and I prayed and prayed and prayed that Harry would be the one man to survive these insurmountable odds.

Around 7:00 a.m., I went back to Harry's room to check on him before heading home. I wanted to be there at home when Harrison woke up. Harry was heavily sedated and there was no change in his condition or the way he looked. The rest of the family left then as well to go get some much-needed sleep. When my dad parked in front of our house,

Batzi came out to get her newspaper. She asked how Harry was doing and my dad began sobbing, struggling through telling the story of what had happened through the night. Batzi lovingly took charge, telling my dad to get my mom and go home to get some sleep, that she would stay with me and with Harrison for as long as we needed.

When she came in, she sat down and said, "I'm not leaving. I want to be here for you. Just pretend I'm not here—go ahead and do what you need to do, but I don't want you to be alone." I quietly told her all of the details of what had happened and the dire resultant prognosis. She must have gone through half a box of Kleenex, but I was so stunned, exhausted and discouraged by the prognosis, I don't remember shedding many tears. I kept thinking that I was telling this horrible story about some other family. Thankfully, we had just finished talking about all of the scary details by the time Harrison woke up, but when he walked into the kitchen and saw the two of us, he was very frightened. He immediately asked if Harry was okay and I told him that he had had major surgery last night and that he was alive but very, very sick. I knew that I would tell him everything at some time in the future, but I knew, too, that this was not the time.

After posting the above update at 9:30 a.m., I was finally able to get a couple hours of sleep before heading back to the hospital. And, true to her word, Batzi did not leave all day, until she drove Harrison to practice and I left for the hospital.

As you can imagine, responses to my morning July 31 email were somber, stunned, sober messages.

"Oh, my God.... How can this be happening? I can't stop my tears. I have no words...."
~BH

"I wish I were there to put my arm around your shoulder.... You must be so tired after all the strain, hope, terror, hope and relief, then fear again. Please know that everyone is praying hard for Harry to pull himself up over that last hill to recovery. We all love him and believe if anybody can do it, he can."
~KW

*"If anyone can make it through this journey, it is Harry.
Your emails are going all over the country, to friends of
Harry's. EVERYONE is praying and praying for his survival
and recovery. He is a man respected, admired and loved and
thousands are pulling for him."*
~RL

*"I woke up this morning feeling sorry for myself because I
didn't sleep well and have a headache. Then, I read your email
and your tragedy puts everything in perfect perspective for
me. I am numb with sadness for you. I won't stop praying,
praying, praying...."*
~DB

*"After reading your email this morning, I was overwhelmed
with the thought that God wasn't saving Harry, He was trying
to take him because He has a very special place for Harry—in
His loving care and right next to Him. It is Harry who fought
hard to come back to be with you and Harrison and to do more
good works here on earth."*
~MM

*"I don't even know where to start. I cried when I read your
email, I'm crying now. I can't begin to imagine what you are
going through. I'm praying for my friend who inspires me to
be a better man."*
~DC

*"I ... I don't have the right words.... You know I am here for
you and praying so hard. I am tortured by this latest turn of
events, so I cannot begin to imagine how you feel. This is ...
Oh, I just don't even know what to say...."*
~VB

*"Our prayers will bring Harry through this; I just know it. He
is a tough guy, always has been and his spirit is not yet ready
to leave this world."*
~RF

"Holy #$%^. We all thought Harry was out of the critical state. I just got off my knees after saying a prayer and I never pray. I have tears running down my face and I am just devastated by this news. I still choose to believe that HARRY WILL PREVAIL. BELIEVE IN HARRY. You must continue to be strong for him, for Harrison and for yourself.
BELIEVE IN HARRY. BELIEVE IN HARRY. BELIEVE IN HARRY. BELIEVE IN HARRY. BELIEVE IN HARRY. BELIEVE IN HARRY. BELIEVE IN HARRY. BELIEVE IN HARRY. BELIEVE IN HARRY. BELIEVE IN HARRY. BELIEVE IN HARRY. BELIEVE IN HARRY. BELIEVE IN HARRY. BELIEVE IN HARRY. BELIEVE IN HARRY. BELIEVE IN HARRY."
~SS

Friday, July 31, 2009 11:03 p.m.

Harry is Hanging in There

Harry is holding his own tonight. He looks so much better! The swelling and redness in his face have diminished, and he actually looks like himself. His vital signs have been mostly stable throughout the day. He has been pharmaceutically paralyzed because the doctors want absolutely no movement from him. His kidneys are beginning to fail, which is apparently not unexpected at this point. He has been put on dialysis to assist his kidneys until they are able to take over full function again.

He went back to the OR for the replacing of sponges in the abdomen. The surgeon found one more bleeder and tied it off, and is pleased with the slight reduction in the swelling of the organs. They still have a way to go to return to a more normal size so they can close his abdomen. His tummy looks like he is six months pregnant. More of the same is expected for tomorrow and the next day.

In the midst of all this numbing heartache, I found it such a relief today to laugh a few times. A dear friend of Harry's was looking at him today, and leaned over to say, "You know what pisses me off about you, Harry? You've been flat on your back in this bed for nine days, and your hair still looks better than mine!"

Good-night!
Cathy

"I struggle to find words to describe how I'm feeling right now. Just know that the fervent prayers never stop for the three of you. God has carried Harry and your family this far, and He will continue by your sides."
~DB

"You are such an inspiration. Don't let anyone ... doctor or otherwise shake your faith. Harry can feel your energy the most and I know that is what keeps him fighting. I can't wait for him to walk out of the hospital. He will be the one patient that all the doctors and nurses refer to, as the one who

overcame all the odds. He'll be the one they always think of in extreme circumstances. I agree with so many others that have shared with you that Harry is not finished here, and has so much more to do ... he's only just begun."
MF

"Harry is the finest man I know."
~BH

"It's been said by many great doctors that the patients who beat the odds are those who are surrounded by positive, happy, encouraging, loving people. Keep the faith and thank the Lord for all He has done for Harry already."
~CG

"I didn't know about anything that was happening with Harry until last night, when a friend forwarded me your emails. I just sat and cried and cried and cried. I have never known such a fine human being as Harry. I want to extend my sympathy for what you have been going through and my encouragement for Harry's recovery. God works in amazing ways."
~Bill S

"My wife and I have sat here in tears at last night's news and I was unable to even reply. Half a day later and I can barely eat. Hang in there, Cat. I just flashed on one of my favorite pictures, the kitty hanging on the horizontal pole by his paws. I'm sure that is you."
~PC

Saturday, August 1, 2009 11:06 p.m.

Harry is Slightly Better

Harry is more stable and doing better today. He is completely off the paralyzing medication, and is now under regular sedation. He opened his eyes three times today, but is too far under yet to follow a command. His blood pressure has been stable, and all of his vitals have improved since he went on the dialysis machine last night to compensate for the failing of his kidney function. The blood drainage from the abdomen is only half of what it was through the night. His nurse has spent the day making constant adjustments to all of his meds and systems, and she has been busy! Everyone is relieved that he seems to be doing better. He looks really good today—just like he is napping. And, his hair, of course, is ... gorgeous!

I spoke with the nurse about how long we can expect Harry to be hospitalized. I wasn't looking to hold her to a time line, but I am starting to take over some of the duties that Harry normally does for our family, and I need to know for how long I will be doing this, and how much I need to be doing. She was very hesitant to come up with an amount of time, so when I asked her if it was safe to assume that Harry would be hospitalized for at least another month, she said that was a safe assumption. I don't care *how* long he is in the hospital, as long as he leaves it on two feet, not in a box!

In an attempt to reiterate to me what a serious condition Harry is in, the surgeon today told me that over the years, he has only had two other patients in the same situation that Harry now finds himself. Neither of them survived. He also told me that if there is another bleeding incident like this, Harry has no chance of survival. Having an open abdomen is very, very serious, and Harry is extremely sick. *So*, I have nicknamed Harry "Dr. 33 1/3 %" because he is going to be his doctor's one survivor of those three patients. Harry is very strong, he has an incredible will to live, and as so many of you have said, "Harry is not yet done with his service here on earth."

The photo below is on the wall above my desk. Every night, as I write these emails, I look up at that photo. Some nights, I wonder if I will ever see Harry smile like that again. But, when I read your emails of support, when I read about what you love about Harry, when I read about the enormous volume of prayers you are sending our way, I am strengthened. Then, I look up at this picture, and I think, "I can't *wait* to see Harry smile like that again!"

Dr. 33 1/3 %'s Wife

"Dear Dr. 33 1/3%'s wife! I find myself hitting the 'receive emails' button all day long these days to see if there is an update from you. I'm always hoping to see an encouraging subject line. I share your update with my husband and he immediately drops whatever he's doing to listen to me read it to him. We have everybody here on the East Coast praying for Harry. For some reason your email today brought me to tears....I'm so touched by your strength and courage and I feel so much pain in my heart for what you all are going through. It's so difficult to be three thousand miles away—I wish I were there to help you do something. By the way— Harry does have some great hair!"

~LN

"Harry is one of the most kind, energetic, youthful, and most importantly, RESPECTED fellows in Orange County whom I've had the good fortune to know. Dear God I pray that he will pull through this and if anyone can do it, Harry is up to the task. Know that you, Harry, and your entire family are in our daily prayers. If there's anything at all that we can do to lighten the load, please call or email."
~LO

"Yes it's true—Harry has great hair! We're glad to hear some positive news today. He is not finished here on earth. God has more work for him to do—I am absolutely sure of it."
~JD

"Every day I hold my breath before I open my emails to see what remarkable feat Harry has accomplished. And every day I am surprised at how strong he is. Now I know for sure he is a survivor."
~SV

"My GOD ... you have been through so much....You are all on my heart and in my prayers....I wish I could fix this for you.... Keep the faith, stay strong and use your power of love and strength, knowing it is on your side."
~KG

"My heart breaks for you and all that you have had to experience these last few days. I find myself, throughout each day, stopping what I'm doing and having a little talk with God on Harry's behalf. I keep reminding Him of all the great things Harry has done for everyone, never expecting anything in return but because it's out of the goodness of his heart. He is such a kind, loving person and I will continue to make my little stops throughout the day to have a talk with God and ask for another good day tomorrow and the day after and the day after...."
~DA

45

"There is NO Way I see Harry's life being done already. We will celebrate his survival and his total recovery. It will take a while, but it will happen. Cathy, YOU ARE NOT ALONE!! I love you and ache with you. You are in my thoughts, prayers and heart twenty-four hours a day."
~Your Birthday Twin

"Harry has a lot more positive motivation and example-setting to do, (at least for MY son) before he ever leaves this pop stand! So you go tell Dr. 33 1/3% that we've all had enough of his lying around and now it's time to get back to business."
~JM

"I can sleep happy now that I know Harry's hair is gorgeous! For a while, I thought it would have been disrupted ... and for Harry, this simply would not do. I know that soon we will be seeing Harry's smile beaming as we all recount with him the events of these past few days. So I say, 'Dr. 33 1/3%, you have seen how much we all love you. Now come on, get better and let us tell you in person.'"
~PH

"Every time I see an email from you, I hold my breath. This email makes me relax because it sounds so encouraging, although I know he is still in very critical condition. This makes us all realize how fragile our lives are and we thank you deeply for keeping us all informed. We think of your family so many times a day, it is impossible to count."
~SK

Sunday, August 2, 2009 8:44 p.m.

A Restful Day with Slight Improvement

Today was a quiet, restful day for Harry. We are so grateful that he has made it through the past two days without any complications or setbacks. His blood pressure has been stable all day—a good sign! Yesterday, he needed 95-100% oxygen concentration, and he will eventually need to get down to 35%. By mid-day today, he was at 40%. His nurse was thrilled!

Early this morning, Harry's nurse, Caroline (another fabulous nurse) took his sedation down so she could check his responses. When she asked him if he was in pain, he slowly nodded yes. He opened his eyes briefly, and tried to lift his arms. Caroline was pleased with the results, then put him back into la-la land. He has been heavily sedated since then, and has rested comfortably all day. He is still on dialysis.

Family members have taken turns with Harry most of the day, rubbing his hands and feet, talking to him, *admiring his hair*! It's been peaceful and hopeful.

Last week, I ran into our friend, Katy, in the CICU waiting room. She is a cardiac telemetry ICU nurse at the hospital (Cardiac telemetry is the next step that Harry will go to after leaving CICU). She was so shocked to hear that I was there for Harry, who had been her son's baseball coach for two years. When I saw her today, she told me that when she saw Harry's surgeon last week after we chatted, she told him, "Of all the patients you've ever had, if you are going to save *anyone*—it has to be *this* man!" Love that woman!!!

Expecting another better day tomorrow,
Cathy

As my friend, Jeff, so accurately pointed out, I do suffer a bit from that Superwoman Complex. I think I can and should do everything myself, and truth be told, I also love to be in control. But it was right about now that I realized I wanted and needed to begin accepting offers of help from friends and family, and I had thousands of offers! I knew that Harry might spend another month in the hospital … if he made it …

and there were already so many demands on my time. It was liberating to give friends a job to do. It helped me and it helped them. Friends wanted to do SOMETHING. They couldn't heal Harry, but the next best thing was to support me, Harrison, and Harry's family. I thought back on the times when I have had friends in need and how wonderful it is to contribute to the welfare of the family while they face their challenges. Friends provided food, company, advice, driving, dog-walking, flowers, car-washing, house cleaning ... you name it, I had it. Every single thing, big, small, or somewhere between, was a gift for which I will always be grateful. So often in the years since 2009, when I think about the benevolence of so many that summer, I am immediately reminded of one of my favorite John Wooden quotes, "You can't have a perfect day until you do something for someone who will never be able to repay you."

"Hi Wife of Dr. Great Hair!
Two or three days of peace and serenity for Harry is super.
It surely helps you too, Cathy, doesn't it? Perhaps this time
we've really turned the corner regarding Harry's fight for
health. Your reports do reflect a better frame of mind and that
must be reflective of what you see in Harry. You have been
on such an awful roller coaster ride but I want you to know
that we have been on this awful ride with you and Harrison.
We appreciate your diligent postings, keeping everyone in the
loop, as we pray from afar and await more good news."
~Bill S

"I was so shocked and saddened to hear of Harry's heart
issues and hospitalization. I went to see him this afternoon,
thinking he would be well on his way to recovery. I entered
his room and stopped in my tracks, as I was struck by the
severity of his condition. Unconscious, hooked up to a dozen
lines and machines. After a minute the nurse asked if I was a
family member and when I told her no, that I am a colleague
of his, she asked me to leave. I'm so sorry that I did that—I
had no idea what grave condition he is in and that he was not
supposed to have visitors. I'm very, very sorry for the intrusion.

Harry's condition is quite sobering. I am sorry that your family is going through this horrific ordeal. Harry is strong and he's a fighter and I know he will survive."
~FW

"Dear Mrs. 33 1/3,
Every morning, the first question I get from my family is, 'Did you get a Harry update yet?' Everyone in our family is praying for Harry's recovery. God only knows how many countless other fans are in the wings praying for his return to health."
~LM

"We are in AWE of this amazing story....It DOES NOT SEEM REAL. It will be even more amazing when the heavenly and earthly angels bring Harry back home to you and his family."
~RE

"Every time I read one of your emails, the tears just flow. Bad news or good news, this is so unbelievable and overwhelming. Anything you need, my dear, you just ask.... "
~GM

"You know ... The 'Big Dodger in the Sky' has a lot more for Harry to do here on earth."
~DA

"It's so wonderful to hear that things are looking better. I'm beginning to think the number '3' has something going for Harry. A week ago I told my husband I was naming Harry 'Harry the Cat.' By my estimation, at the time, he had possibly used three of his nine lives. Didn't know his name for you was Cat, which (by the way) has three letters. And you came up with Dr. 33 1/3%. I'm sure a numerologist would have a party with this one! I really don't care what anyone wants to believe in as long as it keeps Harry here with all the people who love him so much. I even considered selling my husband to the devil, but I'm sure the devil would give him back! Thank goodness because I love that man of mine, just as you love

yours!"
~Barb S

Our friend Jeff told me that his son came into his room at 2:00 a.m. this day, saying that he just woke up and was thinking about how tough all of this has been on Harrison, so he wrote him this letter:

"Harrison …

About five months ago I was put into the same situation you are in now. I can only imagine what you are feeling now because I was there … in the same position you stand in today. All I can say to you is be strong and do what your dad always wanted you to do.

Keep working hard and keep doing the best you can in all things, just as you were taught. To make the pain less, keep your mind set on something … maybe a goal or maybe just indulge yourself into activities and good-spirits. Never give up … always fight on and pursue what you really want. When my dad was in the hospital it was around the end of the school year and the way I kept my mind off of things was working hard at school. It's summer now but find something you love to do and just keep doing it. Work hard and make your dad proud like you know he would want you to do. You're a great kid, and I know you will get through this … Don't worry,

—your friend and pal, PR
Peace, lil bud"

Monday, August 3, 2009 12:24 p.m.

Blood Donations in Harry's Name

Thank you to those of you who have offered to donate blood. Harry has had thirty-six units of blood since he first was admitted to the hospital twelve days ago. At this moment, he is in surgery again and it wouldn't be surprising to see him need more over the next couple of days.

The hospital would greatly appreciate blood donations to help replenish their supply. Harry would be honored to have you donate in his name. He is type A positive, but it doesn't matter what type you have. The hospital would appreciate any donations of all types.

Thank you so much!

Cathy

Monday, August 3, 2009 10:41 p.m.

Stable and Improving Slightly

Regarding my email earlier in the day, I would request that if you are interested in donating blood, please make an appointment with the Donor Lab at the hospital, so that you don't have to wait. Many of you donated already today! Thank you!

Late this morning, Harry went back to the OR and his doctor was pleased with the lack of bleeding. The abdomen will remain open for several more days, because the internal organs are still quite swollen. He's hoping to begin slowly closing the incision on Wednesday, and complete it over the next few days.

Harry is still on dialysis, but the doctors expect at this point that he will eventually regain function. It may be weeks, but they are hopeful. He has been on a respirator for a long time, so to avoid further complications, he will most likely have a tracheotomy later this week. Still of concern is the compromised function of each internal organ. We have a way to go, but we are making positive progress.

Sheila was back today! She told me that she called the nurses every day to check on Harry. When she heard what happened Thursday night, she was stunned and said she hasn't stopped praying for him since that dreadful night.

All of Harry's vital signs remained stable today. He is really beating the odds, surprising the doctors. But we aren't surprised by that, are we? Harry is young, healthy, and strong. He's fighting hard to come back to us. We are expecting him to improve slowly and rest well over the next few days.

Writing these updates is soothingly therapeutic for me every night. Also, this is a journal for Harry. He doesn't know what's happening to him! Can you imagine how disbelieving he will be about all of this?!? He's been under sedation for twelve days now, and will be so for many more days. When he is up to it, he will be able to read about what happened. I'm also printing all of the emails you have sent to us. One of the few things he will be able to do in the early days of recovery is read—and he will be busy! Your cute stories, your notes of encouragement, your compassion for our family, your thoughts of love and friendship, your offers of help and prayer will overwhelm him and help him heal.

Thank you for everything you all have done for us....
Cathy, Harry, and Harrison

I mention in this update that writing the emails and posts were therapeutic for me. They were indeed, although as I look back, I believe they were absolutely essential for my well-being. Once I documented what happened and how I felt, I knew I could "decompress," as my friend Tina so aptly put it and let it go to "re-fill my gas tank" of energy and emotion. Nobody knew, at this point, how long Harry would be unconscious or how much he would even know or remember about what had happened to him. It became a journal that I eventually shared with Harry. Every year, on the anniversaries of certain dates ... July 23, July 31, September 5, November 25 ... we re-read the journal entries of what transpired on those particular dates. Those entries never fail to amaze me. I lived through it all, but there are little snippets here and there that I have forgotten and most importantly, stories that I will never forget. Having the journal helps me, for the millionth time, realize how fortunate we are that this story eventually had the ending that it did.

Tuesday, August 4, 2009 10:39 p.m.

Day Thirteen

Thank you to those of you who have donated blood and have
made appointments! Yesterday, when a friend called to make her
appointment, the donor lab scheduling nurse said, "Who *IS* this
Dr. White?!?! I've never seen this much outpouring of support!"
Several people at the hospital today already thanked me, so I
pass the thanks along to you—from the hospital, from the White
family!!

Harry had a very stable day today. Through the night, he had
a few tremors, so a neurologist ordered an EEG to check to see
if the tremors were from seizures. We don't have the results yet,
and there were no more tremors during the day, so the docs aren't
worried. Everything else looked good all day. He continues to be
heavily sedated, and looks comfortable, out of pain.

The vascular surgeon examined Harry tonight while I was
with him and he told me that he has scheduled Harry to go to the
OR tomorrow mid-day to begin closing the abdomen!! He is very
encouraged, told me that this is earlier than most patients would
be ready to begin the closing process. Probably the following
day, he will have the tracheotomy done, and then continue on
consecutive days of surgery until the abdomen is completely
closed.

I had a very lengthy discussion this morning with Harry's
cardiologist. We went over every detail of each day since Harry
was brought in early that Thursday morning when he was first
admitted to the hospital. When he explained the scenario that
led up to the placement of the second stent, he said that that very
same thing had not happened with any of his patients in well
over 10 years, that the occurrence is about one in 100,000! The
bleeding incident this past Thursday is even more rare—in fact,
he has never seen anything like it. A couple of times, he said, "If
he makes it through the next two weeks, we will...." The second
time he said that, I put my hand on his arm, and said, "I'm quite
certain you meant to say, *WHEN* he makes it through the next
two weeks." He smiled and said, "If anybody can, it will be
Dr. White. He's very strong, he's a fighter. But, let's not even

mention the ugly word ... complication."
  Today was Day thirteen—but it was not at all unlucky!
Cat

"If I can give Harry some of my feistiness and stubbornness
from my blood, he will be up and badgering those doctors in
no time! I can't wait to tease him and he will take it as good-
naturedly as he always does. This Thanksgiving we will have
so much to be grateful for—I'll drop off a good bottle of wine,
give you both a hug and then turn around and deck Harry
for scaring the living s#@& out of all of us. Harry feels your
strength and optimism and it's keeping him fighting. With each
day, there will be more healing. Slow and steady, and maybe
a setback here or there. In the end, he will be restored to full
health, and oh, what a celebration we will have!"
~MF

"I can't wait to give Harry a hard time that he has some
of my blood flowing in him.... it may be detrimental to his
hair!!"
~MT

"The only reason there weren't double the number of donors
is that a legion of friends of Harry's live far away. Now at
least the hospital staff understands WHO they are dealing
with here ... And they will soon realize why Dr. 33 1/3 is still
with us. I think of Harry all throughout every day and say
a little prayer each time. It's usually something like this ...
'Please God, Harry has more good to do on this earth, so put
Your healing hands on him, make him well again and let him
get back to serving his family, his friends and his community.
There really aren't enough men like him for the rest of us to
rely on, don't you agree, Lord?' I hope He doesn't mind a little
friendly suggestion from me at least ten times a day."
~KW

"What we have learned and obviously what you have learned is that life is very fragile and the passage of time is fleeting. All we can do about it in the end is to love each other, our family, our friends and to try to enjoy and cherish every passing moment we have with them. In the blink of an eye, it can all change and vanish forever."
~RP

"Cathy, I just had a good cry for you and have been thinking about the three of you constantly. I can relate to so much of what you say. The reality of Harry's medical care and those heavy decisions about taking over the day-to-day things that he normally does—it's overwhelming. I always told Jeff that he had to get better cuz I didn't want to be in charge anymore. Paying bills, running the business, looking for the money tree—too much to do on top of being his advocate at the hospital. But I never missed him more than when I had to lock up the house at night, something he always does. I know you're wondering, 'Am I going to do this for the rest of my life?' Then, you have to be the attentive, positive mom. There is a switch in us women that just goes into survival mode and we just do what needs to be done. You can do it but be sure to take care of yourself because you are needed to take care of everyone else. Harry will get well and before you know it, he will be walking around locking up the house for the night. There will come a time where you look back and think did that really happen?? PLEASE let others help you when they offer or when they ask, tell them what they can do. Delegate whatever you can to relieve the smallest stress off of you. You will be glad you did, as will they."
~JR

"I am at the hospital today for my monthly gawking session. I wish I could relay to you the anxiety that runs through me each and every time I walk through the lobby of the hospital, any hospital. It's not a good feeling yet I should feel great when I do because this is where doctors worked miracles that saved my life. Today, I went in with a new thought. I pretended

I was going to see Hare Dog and that I was not there for me at all. No anxiety, no mental pain—once again Hare Dog made someone feel better, even for just a little while, and he wasn't even there! I hope he gets to read this shortly after he wakes up. I've got to let him know of a downside to a certain situation that I found out about. I wish someone had told me earlier—the foot massages and hand rubbing do not go on for very long after you're able to sit up and talk! It's a bit of a withdrawal situation that I did not at all enjoy! You get used to the attention and affection very quickly and then all of a sudden—POOF—it's gone. Such a bummer...."
~Jeff

"We are all so grateful that you take the time to keep us in the loop on Harry's progress. I think about him at work and at home and when I talk about him with friends. It amazes me how many people know him. From a medical perspective, I agonized hearing the evolution of his medical events. But I kept thinking, if anyone can ride the storm, it is Harry White! Not only is he an incredible guy but he has an incredible family and support network of friends. Please know that your continued optimism is crucial and necessary and will make the medical team caring for him even more diligent in pulling him through this. After this match, I'm sure the hospital staff has prepared you for a prolonged recovery phase to get him back on his feet, but he can do it! With you as his cheerleader, he will indeed be Dr. 33 1/3%!"
~DB

"It is SO inspiring to see Harry's character shine through even though sedated! To the question 'Who is this Harry White?' I would say, 'An outstanding character with family, smile, sense of humor and of course, HAIR, to match!'
We are pulling for you, Harry! Our prayers continue...."
~JK

"I knew day thirteen would be a successful day. Besides, Dr. White can overturn any superstition and prove it to be

something wonderful and glorious as he does just by his nature! Each day we get a number of past patients, current patients and dentists alike who want to show their love, concern and support for 'our' Dr. White and I am proud to be a part of his team here at the office who are rooting for him each day! We don't go to bed until we have heard the updates ... which has given us all something to cheer about when we get together the next day!!! As a side note, when my father slipped into his ten day coma following a bypass, he told me that he could hear people talking around him and it gave him the will to find his way toward the voices he was hearing ... so KEEP TALKING AND LAUGHING AND READING ALL THE FAN MAIL U CAN TO HIM ... I believe he will use this and we will be talking about this at our next Christmas Party! We were never able to top his stories anyway, but this takes the prize, Dr. White! Love you, Cathy and Harrison ... give a hug from me and the girls would ya?"
~BG

"Harry, What is not a surprise is that you have shown everyone what it is to come together as a community ... a family. Hearing about all the blood donors that have flooded the hospital and the friends that have all reassessed their lives and taken personal inventory of the way they live it is awe inspiring. You make me want to be a better person, Harry."
~DA

Wednesday, August 5, 2009 11:16 p.m.

CaringBridge Website

We first learned of the CaringBridge website when our dear friends Gary and Sandy Barker used it. They lost their beautiful son, Christian, to a rare form of leukemia in December 2007. For the twenty months of Christian's treatment, Harry and I checked the website daily to follow Christian's progress.

Last night, the Barkers set up a CaringBridge website for Harry! (Thank you, Gary and Sandy!!!!) As you will see, it provides a great way to read updates, and share stories and comments.

Cathy and the Boys

Thursday, August 6, 2009 11:05 p.m.

The Best Thursday Yet

Harry is definitely doing better today! Early this morning, the tracheotomy was done. It is so much better for Harry to not have that respirator tube down his throat, taped to his mouth. Now, he truly looks like he is sleeping peacefully. He is completely off blood pressure medication, which is a huge step. His vital signs have remained stable all day. His white blood cell count is down, and temp was normal today. The culture results from yesterday's testing will be available tomorrow.

The areas of the stent placements are vulnerable to catching clots. His dialysis filters need to be changed about three times per day, because of clotting. If he were a patient without these complications, he would be using a mild blood thinner to prevent the possibility of a clot catching in the stents. But because internal bleeding has almost killed him—twice—he absolutely cannot have any blood thinners. We've been keeping our fingers crossed that no clots gather in the stent area. If that were to happen, we would start all over with running a catheter to the heart, maybe placing another stent—God forbid. Statistically, the first two weeks after the initial heart incident, the heart is especially vulnerable to another episode. Each week thereafter, the chance drops bit by bit. Today is day fifteen, and it's time to heave a small sigh of relief. We've passed a statistical milestone. The chance of another incident is way below what it was last week at this time. Harry is making progress!

Today, when my brother Rick was donating blood, the nurse, Sharon, said, "I have been here for twenty years and I have never seen anything like this. Even when our community suffers the injury or death of a firefighter or a policeman, the response is not like this. I've booked appointments for weeks to come, and have added another day each week to accommodate the appointments. Usually, only 50 percent of the appointees show up, but for Dr. White—it is 100 percent!!" *Thank you, our friends, for doing this for Harry!*

Tonight, as I looked at Harry's face, it was as if he were going to slowly open an eye and wink at me. He looks good,

considering what he has been through. It struck me for at least the hundredth time in the last two weeks—that I am amazed by and very proud of how strong he is. His strengths—physical, emotional, spiritual—are what have saved him from the hideous complications of the past two weeks—that, and your love, your prayers.
Cathy

"These past few days, I really took the time to let the people in my life know how much I love and appreciate them! This situation has been an eye-opener for me and I'm sure for many others. What a huge sacrifice your family is making for all of us to learn that lesson."
~LD

"I think if Harry woke up now and someone told him what had happened, he would laugh in disbelief. I actually think he wanted to prove that no matter what was thrown at him, his hair would still remain perfect. We are indeed, not worthy."
~PH

"I am in Greece and just got internet for the first time today in the past two weeks. I am so devastated by this horrendous turn of events—I am crying as I type this and cannot stop thinking of my wonderful friend and colleague. Please whisper to him that I will not stop thinking of him or praying for him until he walks out of that hospital."
~SD

"When I went by the lab to donate blood, the technician said, 'Who IS this Harry White?!? We are swamped with donors for him.' So I said, 'If you knew him for just five minutes, you would understand this outpouring of love and concern for him. There are not many people on earth any finer than this man.'"
~SF

"LOVE, LOVE, LOVE to get emails about Harry's slow ascent

back to complete recovery. These emails are SOOOOOOOO
much better than the crazy 'Code Blue' email last Friday! That
one put me in a funk that I'm just now escaping and a big part
of the escape is the daily update from you on Harry's return to
health."
~SS

"As a doctor, I admit that medical technology can only do so
much. As a spiritual woman, I believe the rest is up to the
strength, prayers and support from everyone around Harry.
I don't think he could have survived what he's gone through
without that. Keep it up and let me know if I can help you in any
way."
~T

"We've been friends for how many years—forty? I think back
on the very carefree days of summer we spent together in our
teens and who would ever have imagined that this story would
be a chapter in the novel of your life? We never would've
believed this. I love you, my friend!"
~DM

"I'm going in next week to donate blood, so on the night
before, I'm going to have a bottle of 1987 Caymus Cabernet.
That should fix Harry right up! Keep the faith, I know
everything is going to be okay."
~RR

"Tell Harry this when he wakes up ... A little-known baseball
fact: the first testicular guard (a cup) was used in baseball
in 1874 and the first helmet was used in 1934. It took sixty
years for men to realize that the brain is also important!"
~CD

"Tell Harry that since we share the same birthdate and year,
I DO NOT give him permission to skip this birthday, or any
others ... for a long, long time!"
~GP

"Cat, I remember the day you told us you were pregnant. Those years have flown by in the blink of an eye. Then yesterday, seeing fourteen-year-old Harrison at the hospital, my heart absolutely broke for him. He is so grown up! This is really difficult for him—trying to be so strong and supportive for you, and watching his dad fight for his life. So tough, it tears at my heart. Thank you for letting us see Harry. It was ... very difficult. I don't really have the words to express exactly how I felt when I saw him. Scared, stunned ... it's hard to see the life of the party, a treasured friend, look like he does.

I know the emails you send are very cathartic but I still wonder how you do it. We are all so thankful, however, that you do have the courage to write. The details are important to us. It continues to make it very real, just as it should be, so that every day we have a reality check and take the time to praise and thank God for the smallest blessings we take for granted—like breathing without a tube down our throats. As you would say, 'Don't sweat the small stuff!' This whole ordeal really puts that little phrase into a very necessary perspective. Loving you until my heart hurts,"
~VB

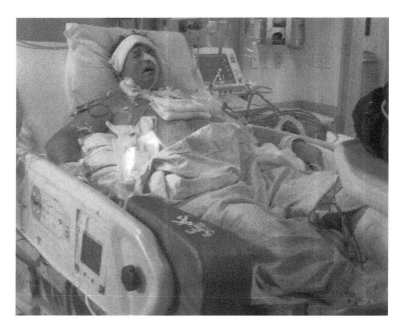

Back from Code Blue

Friday, August 7, 2009 11:38 p.m.

Stable and Improving

Harry's day was restful and uneventful ... cause for celebration in itself!! All of his vital signs remained consistent where we like to see them! His doctors and nurses are very pleased with his progress.

Tomorrow at 1:30 p.m., Harry is scheduled for the next abdominal surgery. The surgeon will close the abdomen a little further, but probably not all the way. He expects that it may be another week before the closures of all layers are complete.

Today was a busy day of meeting with doctors to discuss all of the systems that need to improve—not only for Harry's survival, but so that he doesn't suffer any permanent damage from everything that he has endured over the last 16 days. His kidneys, lungs, internal organs, brain, blood, and heart, still have a long way to go before they are back to normal. But ... what a difference from a week ago! We were all feeling better when we left the hospital tonight—more hopeful than in a long time! Harry has been fighting for his life—and I believe he is winning that fight.... Don't worry about Dr. White—he will be back with us before you know it!

Enjoy your weekend.... Harry would want you to do just that!
Cathy and Harrison

"Even though I am a grown woman now, I will always think of Harry as my twenty-five-year-old cousin, holding a bowl of chocolate chips over my eight-year-old head, asking 'Who's your favorite cousin?' while wearing that winning smile. Whenever in his presence, I've always felt like the most important person in the world. Thank you, Harry, for the kind of love and patience you showed that eight-year-old little girl, and the love and encouragement you still show your grown cousin."
~LH

"July 30, 2009, the bottom of our world fell out ... For many of us, the shock and disbelief that our dear friend Harry White had a serious health battle to wage were frightening and overwhelming. True to form, Harry, you continue to motivate us with your perseverance and will. I look forward to the day to once again work side by side with you creating smiles and happiness, having our 'business meeting' beach hikes, and fireside chats! Cathy, you are a rock. Your strength and clear-headed focus are amazing. You are an inspiration, pure and simple. Harry knows how lucky he is to have you by his side, and we are so indebted to you for keeping the community who cares so much for you, Harry, and Harrison aware of Harry's progress. My family, along with our remarkable staff and their families send our most heart-felt well-wishes."
~CZ

"As I read all the postings from your friends, it seems so odd to me that I have known you two for so long. I knew Cathy before you even started dating each other, yet I really don't know you, Harry, the way your other friends do, because life took me across the country. Reading the postings makes me wish I had gotten to spend more time with you. I cherish the fact that we do keep in touch and I hope the future holds many opportunities to spend time together."
~AG

"We continue to pray for Harry, that God will touch and heal him so he can get home to the family he loves so much. We pray for continued strength for you, Cathy, and for Harrison. I cannot begin to imagine what each day must be like for the two of you. Finally, for Harry's mom and dad ... The glimpses into your family's life at Little League games has been an example to all of us who come in contact with you of a family filled with support and unconditional love and tight bonds from one generation to the next. Harry is blessed to be surrounded by family and friends who love and care for him so much. We all look forward to seeing that smiling face out and about soon."
~HW

65

"There is a saying that you can tell the life people lead by the friends they keep. That saying is perfect for Harry. Look at all the love that is surrounding him."
~JG

"Does anybody else feel like they are living in the Twilight Zone?!?! Day after day, as we read these updates, we shake our heads in disbelief."
~SW

"Remember the TV show "Cheers!"? Here is a quote from Sam Malone, ex-ball player, bartender, 'Good looks opens doors, good hair blows the doors off!' Go for it, Harry—blow the doors off!"
~MM

"Remember this poignant saying: A HEALTHY MAN HAS MANY WISHES .... A SICK MAN HAS ONE!"
~SB

"Every morning, before I read your update, I close my eyes and visualize seeing Harry and Harrison together at school, hugs and 'I love yous' at drop-off or after practice. I see Harry dreaming about playing golf with Harrison while he is in his sedation dreams. I know this will be a reality ... very soon!"
~LF

"Aloha, Cathy, H-man and Dr. Harry,
Sending you many Aloha wishes for a speedy recovery, Harry! Your island buddy is thinking of you daily. You are an Ironman, Harry, and you need to come home soon. I found a dolphin that has 'Amelogenesis imperfecta' and she needs your attention ASAP!"
~PM

Saturday, August 8, 2009 11:50 p.m.

Is It Really Day Seventeen?

It's hard to believe that Harry has been in the hospital for seventeen days. The last time I shared a conversation with him was sixteen days ago at 3:30 in the afternoon! It will be a while longer until we speak, but we are getting closer and closer to that day. Maybe a week? Maybe ten days?

Harry continues to improve. When he went in for the abdominal surgery today, the surgeon was not expecting to be able to close him any further. But he was pleased to see that all the organs look better, and the swelling is slowly receding. So, he did accomplish a bit more closing. Harry tolerated the surgery well, and is still on a low dose of paralytic and a high dose of pain meds to keep him relaxed and comfortable.

Early today, Harry had a CT scan of his brain, as part of the work-up that needed to be done to check for possible neurological damage as a result of all that he has gone through in the last two weeks. Thank God, everything is okay for now. There are no clots, no bleeding, no evidence of stroke, and no excessive fluid accumulation.

So many of you have asked me how Harry's parents are doing. (Harry Sr. is 92 and Helen will be 86 next Thursday.) *They are doing remarkably well!* They have been ... so strong, so full of faith. Of course, it's been difficult for them to watch their child suffer and fight for life. I can only imagine that gripping heartache from a parent's perspective. They have had their moments (as have we all) in the last seventeen days. But they amaze me with their resilience and positive attitude! Harry will be justifiably proud of them when he hears of their devotion and their strength. Now, we know where Harry gets his strength— good genes and a great example set by two wonderful parents! Cathy

"I always think of Harry as "Dr. White", not because of studies, even if he is the representative poster child for orthodontic care. He is a doctor in the sense that he makes

everyone feel loved whenever he smiles and greets you. He makes you feel like family whether he is meeting you for the first time or the thousandth time. We are looking forward to seeing his smile in the very near future."
~MM

"Frickin' Harry—he just never does anything by half measure, does he?"
~DW

"Dr. White, you've been such a positive influence on all the kids at our school, teaching them not just about the physical skills of sports, but also about sportsmanship and the attitude of winners. And you know as well as anyone that athletes like you never quit, never give up. Once you're back on your feet and teaching young athletes again, you're going to be able to relate this experience to them—about fighting in times of adversity, about never giving up, to stay positive, to keep fighting. I'm looking forward to that day again soon, when you'll be flashing your trademark smile and providing the positive support to our kids. We're all rooting for you from the sidelines."
~TM

"Stopped by the CICU yesterday after work to see how you were doing and saw two wonderful things. One, that you were resting peacefully and the second, your wife holding your hand and caressing it gently. I spoke to her for approximately twenty minutes (during which time she never let go of your hand), getting a very thorough and detailed recap of what had transpired in the last two weeks. She was amazingly calm and collected and had the confidence of Dan Marino at the two minute warning in reassuring me that everything is going to be just fine. Of that, I have no doubt and hope that it will be in the very near future. You are respected and loved by everyone who knows you and we sincerely hope the vibrant and energetic Harry comes back to us very soon. Best wishes to a quick recovery to complete health,"
~SF

"Harry, we look forward to the day, hopefully not too far down the road, when you can stand up in front of all of us, at a celebratory party in your honor and quote Mark Twain, 'The reports of my demise have been greatly exaggerated.' We would never have wished this horrific nightmare on you and your beautiful family, but in retrospect, I am reminded of Magic Johnson's fight against HIV. Sometimes God chooses the best and the brightest, the strongest and the bravest, to stand up to, fight back against, and conquer the seemingly invincible foe. You are our warrior and we will all revel in your eventual victory."
~TL

"Cathy, Thank you for letting us visit today. In the hour that we were with Harry, for once, we did ALL the talking. It was nice of Harry not to say a single thing! I'm quite certain he laughed at all my jokes. He looked peaceful, with the odd grimace as the bed moved. But I must admit tears did well up in my eyes. I wanted so desperately for him to open his eyes, sit up and say 'gotcha!' I also wanted him to joke that one of the IV bags actually contained an ice-cold martini. But then I knew it did not when I looked for the 'salad' (green olives) and found none."
~PH

"You must know by now, Cathy, how Harry's illness has impacted SO VERY MANY PEOPLE! There are more prayers and well-wishes coming your way than you can even imagine. And because of the severity of it all, everyone is taking the time to be very cognizant of how precious life is. As you asked us all to do in that very first email, we are hugging tighter, kissing longer and getting on our knees with things more often for all that is dear to us."
~MB

"I know only family is supposed to see Harry, but when you let me see him today, I understood why. The severity of his condition is frightening and many people might lose faith in

69

his survival if they were to see him this way. I am choosing to visualize him as I saw him today, and with each passing day, I will see him in my mind, move closer and closer to recovery and full health. And I would move heaven and earth to help you with ANYTHING you need."
~CR

"I follow your postings every day and I still cannot believe this is happening. Please, somebody, wake me from this horrible nightmare. And, Cathy, eat something, will ya? You are way too skinny!"
~LK

"Your journals and the love that pours out from them for Harry and everyone else inspire me to be a better husband, father and man. Your anecdotes about Harry confirm for me that there is nothing greater for a man to be or do than to be the best husband and father that he can be."
~FR

"Harry, if there was ever someone in life who truly looked to make a positive difference in other people's lives, it is you. It is very evident that God has very special plans for you here on this earth, and that you are faithful to His calling. Thank you for the example you set in our community. Thank you for being such a caring and wonderful human being, for making a difference in so many people's lives. Everyone is anxious to see you come back to us."
~EN

Sunday, August 9, 2009 11:11 p.m.

A Cozy Sunday

Today was a restful day, with more stability. It was a welcome day of healing after the busy day yesterday—two procedures in the same day are tough, especially when one is a surgery. Harry's bilirubin level is elevated today, so the liver is a new concern. There is a slight yellow tinge to his skin, so he will be watched and have his blood tested every six hours, and be examined by yet another specialist.

Harry is cozy beneath a *beautiful* prayer quilt brought to him by a group of dear friends. As each knot was made in the quilt, a prayer was said for Harry. There are six ties in the center of the quilt left for family members to knot after they pray.

Harry's nurse today is a dream! Andrea is so competent, a nurturing sweetheart, and beautiful! I told Harry he needs to wake up so that he can check out his gorgeous nurse. He's missing out. He has a beautiful woman washing his hair, shaving his face, touching his skin ... and he's sleeping through it?!? We'll need to tease him about this in the near future!

On the morning that I came home from the hospital after the hideous Code Blue/CPR/surgery evening, I told Harrison the basics of what had happened. I kept it factual, without the awful details because I didn't want to scare him. Yesterday, someone asked if we thought Harry will come back to tell us that he had an out-of-body experience, and wondered if he might have seen the bright, white light. Harrison overheard the question, and I could see the wheels turning!

Last night, when we got home, Harrison asked me if his dad really came that close to dying and I told him yes. For the first time, I told him every detail of that horrible night—going to the hospital and seeing immediately that Harry wasn't doing well, hearing the Code Blue call for Bed 4, about his call to me shortly after the Code Blue call, being told that Harry probably wouldn't make it and that I should go see him alive for the last time, watching the crew perform CPR. I told him about calling the grandparents and Uncle Bill and Aunt Kathi, and about holding Harry's mom as she cried the heartbreaking cry of a mother who thinks she is losing a child. I told him of my pounding heart as the nurse walked towards us, then my flooding relief when she told us that Harry had a pulse. I told him about being in the waiting room, curled in a chair, watching the sun rise, in a haze of sadness, fear, and exhaustion, wondering what the day would bring. I told him about seeing how battered Harry looked after almost forty-five total minutes of CPR. I told him how relieved I felt as I walked out into the fresh morning air, knowing that I would be telling Harrison that his dad was still alive. Harrison's eyes widened and his jaw dropped a few times during the story. When I finished he said, "Okay, Mom ... Dad is NEVER going to believe this!!"

Harrison has done remarkably well over the last eighteen days. He is strong and calm, and has never doubted that Harry would make it. What bothers him is seeing Harry suffer. In the last year, he has expressed an interest in becoming a doctor, so he enjoys learning about everything that is going on with Harry. He isn't squeamish about blood draws, or IV drips, and has courageously checked out Harry's abdomen, which is still open several inches!

In between visits to the hospital, I've kept Harrison busy and distracted as much as possible. He goes to football practice from 4:00 p.m. to 7:30 p.m. every weekday, and he spent one week doing community service for school. He's been at this school since preschool, and I could not design a better environment for him to be spending time during this ordeal. This is not just our school, it is our extended family, one that has enveloped us with loving arms of support, generous offers of help, and unending faith. I'm overwhelmed by the gracious, genuine concern of the faculty, staff, parents and students here. I can't thank them enough for helping me feel that we are not alone in this.

"H-Man" has been such a source of comfort and companionship for me. He's been a wonderful help around the house. His sense of humor has provided me with much needed smiles and laughter. The toughest part for both of us now, is that *we miss Harry*. Never before have either of us gone eighteen days without talking to or laughing with Harry!! We miss his hugs and kisses, his vibrancy, his humor, his leadership of our family. I could go on and on here—you know I could—there are so many things we miss about Harry. We're lucky, though—it's only a matter of time before we will enjoy being with him again.

Thank you, Diane, for the passage you sent today....

Philippians 4:13 "For I can do everything with the help of Christ who gives me the strength I need."

Until tomorrow,
Cathy

"I am so happy to hear Harry's positive progress. I can't help but smile every time I read the journal you are keeping for him and look forward to getting that phone call from Harry saying, 'Guess what we were doing three years ago today?!'"
~SM

"Harry ... I am reminded daily, through these comments, of how many people you have positively affected in your life. I have always told my children that is a true sign of success in this world! You are an example of how positive energy focused on others makes a lasting impact and I believe your job here is not done. You will continue to inspire with your smile, and your recent experience will now help you to fill others with the hope and faith they might need to navigate through their own difficult times."
~CG

"Harry, I believe you are a miracle in the making! After losing my father and my brother, I also lost my faith. But, your fortitude and fight for survival are renewing my faith like never before."
~JD

"Harry & Cathy, my prayers are with you both, each and every day. As so often happens, we sometimes lose track of certain people who have been in our lives, and it is when particular news travels that we remember how these people were a part of our lives. And that certain 'special' people give

you the ability to instantly re-connect to all those wonderful yesterdays; talking, laughing, sharing stories and hitting tennis balls.... I want to let you both know how much I will enjoy that time when it comes, that we will talk and laugh and share stories again, and if persuaded, perhaps even hit tennis balls."
~JJ

"I have thought of that so many times myself! Harry will have a difficult time comprehending what has happened to him. I cannot imagine waking up, having missed twenty or thirty days of my life."
~NM

"What a joy to read this entry about your son that we love so much! I have no doubt that if he does decide to become a doctor, he will be the compassionate kind that this world so desperately needs! Just a reminder that your Kentucky cousins love you all very much and we thank you for your honest journal entries, and for sharing your heart along with the updates on Harry. It is a beautiful thing."
~LH

Monday, August 10, 2009 Midnight

Quiet and Restful

Today was quiet and moderately restful. Harry now cannot have too high a dose of pain meds, because of his liver (pain meds are metabolized in the liver, bilirubin is still elevated). So, the day was a bit more uncomfortable at times. He grimaced quite a bit today, but didn't respond when we asked if he was in pain. He has a higher dose of relaxant, which is not quite as much of a strain on his liver.

Harry developed a fever through the night—not a surprise, as it is the most common complication of patients in his situation. He has an infectious disease specialist who has taken cultures of every possible source of infection—lungs, IV locations, Foley catheter, etc., and he has been taking them each day for the last eleven days. So far, everything is negative, except for two bacteria in the lungs. Harry is on a very broad spectrum of antibiotics, so this infection should be manageable. Thanks to that prayer quilt, we could cozily tuck Harry in whenever he was chilled from the fever.

There are no plans yet for the next closing of the abdomen, but it appears that the internal organs have lost most of their swelling, so closing may be completely accomplished by the end of the week. That will be a major step—one that will jump-start the function of the internal organs.

It seems that every time we talk about how many days are left in the hospital stay, the time gets longer! It's been almost three weeks now, and we are probably looking at four to five more weeks. All I can say is, thankfully, my husband provided his family with good medical insurance!!!

I'm off to bed so that I can be at a very early morning meeting with our doctors tomorrow. Harrison may be able to sleep in, but I cannot!

Cathy

At this point, knowing that it could still be weeks until Harry would leave the hospital, I began considering moving Harry to a hospital that was closer and more convenient for family members and friends. In addition, several of our personal friends were physicians and staff members at that hospital. One in particular, a neurologist, was especially concerned about Harry's neuro-physical functions and asked me for updates every day. It was becoming more and more difficult to get Harry to respond to stimuli when sedation was reduced, and our friend was extremely concerned about possible brain damage. If anything could be done to help Harry in that regard, our dear friend was desperate to do so. He said that the desire to help save Harry's life was what he would feel if it were his own brother in this same situation.

Moving a patient to another ICU unit is no easy task. A bed must be available and doctors must be willing to take on the patient. Thankfully, our friends were very willing. The bigger issue was finding a spot available. When one did open up, we chose to move him, not knowing how long it might be before another bed became available. We were welcomed with open arms, from friends who were extremely grateful for the opportunity to help us and help bring Harry back to health. It was wonderful—like coming home and just the positive boost that we very much needed.

Tuesday, August 11, 2009 Midnight

A Move Across Town ...

Today, Harry was moved to another hospital. He hasn't had any complications or set-backs, rather this is a positive move to surround Harry with a team of specialists who will help him not only survive, but survive with little or no permanent damage from all that he has endured over the past twenty days. Many of these specialists are personal friends.

Harry still has a low-grade fever, and the bilirubin level from his liver is excessive. His kidneys continue to be of concern, and it is not known at this point if their function will ever return. But he was removed from the twenty-four-hour dialysis, and will go to regular dialysis for only two hours each day—a big step. Tomorrow, he will have the wound evacuation system changed, but no further closure is expected yet. Complete closure is not expected for at least a week. Once the abdomen is closed, it is possible to see the organs "come back to life." We will see what affect the closure will have on the liver and kidneys, in particular.

Once again, I find myself feeling immensely grateful that my family is a part of our school and church community. Several friends from school are the doctors that are now part of Harry's new team at this hospital, and they are an impressive group. Lots of 'ists'—cardiologist, intensivist, nephrologist, neurologist, hematologist.... Tonight, Harry's brother, Bill, my brother, Rick, and I sat with three of Harry's new doctors, and talked about the expectations and challenges of the next several weeks. It will take some time to get Harry back to health, but that is to be expected after the ordeals of the last twenty days. They are hopeful, and so are we!
Cathy

"I am certain that God's perfect plan is at work in all of this. You see, Harry, He knows you and knows that you will be welcomed home when the time is right....But somewhere in the mix there is someone that He needs to touch, to awaken. Harry, it has been this near tragedy that has drawn

so many people together—parents, brothers, friends, hospital employees and more. Somewhere in that mix, a soul is to be saved. He has thrown a lifeline to someone ... through you! What a joy that must be to all involved here! To know that someone was redeemed through this travail will make your journey back to full prosperity a permanent testimony to His glory, as well as your standing with Him."
~DB

Wednesday, August 12, 2009 Midnight

Steps of Progress

Several steps were made today, that though small, are getting Harry closer and closer to rapid improvement. He only had three hours of dialysis today. His own kidneys are still working, though very sluggishly, but this is great news. If his kidneys hadn't been working at all since that awful night when he coded, and after five doses of angiogram dye, there would be virtually no chance of them regaining function. Time will tell, but the nephrologist is hopeful.

It's such a comfort to have the personal connection of friends taking care of Harry. Today, the vascular surgeon took Harry into surgery to exchange the wound evacuation, and was pleased to see that the abdomen was ready to be closed even further—about 50% of the space that was left. Harry tolerated the surgery well, but was fairly uncomfortable *after* the surgery. A couple of doses of morphine and Ativan helped and by the time I left him at 8:30 tonight, he was resting much more comfortably. His skin has a slight yellow tinge yet. Tomorrow, the docs are hoping to begin feeding him through a tube, which will help with all of the recovery, but especially the liver. No procedures (except for dialysis—brought to him in his room) are scheduled for tomorrow, so Harry will have another day to rest and heal.

Harry's brother, Bill, flew home to Colorado tonight. He has been here for twenty days. His beautiful bride of six months (the other Kathi White) went home last weekend. Now that we believe Harry will survive, it is time for Bill to go home to Kathi, and to focus on his own professional and personal duties. He will return in a couple of weeks, but he leaves confident that Harry is in good hands and on his way to recovery.

I had the biggest lump in my throat when Bill said good-bye. Now, as I sit here and think about everything he has done for us in the last three weeks, I'm overwhelmed with emotion. *I don't know what I would have done without him.*

So much about Bill reminds me of what I love about Harry. He's smart and strong, but gracious. I trust him. He's a man of his word. He's extremely generous. He has a good sense of

> humor and a quick laugh. For all of his outward strength and courage, he is tender-hearted. He would do anything for his family. *Thank you, Billy—I love you!*
> Cathy

From my sister-in-law, "The other Kathi White … "

"Dear, dear Cathy,
Although it is so good to have my Bill back home with me today, it pales in comparison to the overwhelming gratitude of hope and joy that I'm feeling in my heart for Harry's continuing progress. You are a sister and brother-in-law that I've known for just a short while, but that I've come to love so much, along with your awesome son, Harrison. Last month you spent just a couple of days here with us in our 'Colorado world' in celebration, but you touched literally hundreds with your warmth and smiles. They constantly ask for Harry and have been praying for him without stopping … armies of them, I tell you! I had the pleasure of meeting so many of your wonderfully supportive friends in the time I spent with you in California last week. I'll never forget them, and look forward to seeing them again. Bill and I will be back soon … we want to see our brother sitting up, talking, and laughing in disbelief at the stories we will tell him. I can just see him now … eyes popping, jaw dropped, slapping the side of his face. In the meantime, Cathy, stay as strong, and as brave, as you are. God will guide you as He wills.
Much Love,"
~The OKW

"I love Billy, too, and I don't even know him! Isn't it wonderful that when tragedy strikes, we find out just who we can count on?! What a blessing families are. The whole "blood is thicker" doesn't always hold true in such terrible times, but it did for you with your wonderful brother-in-law Billy! I'm sure you always suspected he would be there for your family and what an added blessing to find out your faith in him was true."
~GS

"We are holding Harry and your family in prayer many times per day, every day. You two were so good to us when our son was battling cancer. It is our hope that we and everyone else can send that good energy back to you. We know how draining this is as you settle in for the battle. You learn things about yourself that you wish you didn't have to learn. It is a journey and test of strength and fortitude for which you can never prepare. Stay strong and please take time for yourself. Harry is an inspiration and we just KNOW that he will be home soon and you will be a family again."
~JC

Thursday, August 13, 2009 11:56 p.m.

Harry's Mom's Birthday Today

There were lots of positive steps made today. Harry's kidneys are beginning to produce a little more urine on their own! He had dialysis for three hours again today, but the increase by his own body is such great news. Harry received his first nutrition in three weeks today. He has a feeding tube that will finally provide him with the nutrients to begin healing faster, and hopefully, to help his liver return to healthy function.

Harry opened his eyes many times today, turned his head, moved his legs and arms. When his eyes are open, they aren't focused, but a few times today, I could see them try to focus on my eyes and face, if only briefly. He still isn't responding to commands, because of the build-up of sedation medications that have not been able to be metabolized by his kidneys and liver. The docs think it may be four to six more days before that will happen. There are no immediate plans to close the abdomen the remainder of the way. For the next several days, we want Harry to just rest and let his body recuperate.

Today was Harry's Mom's 86th birthday. Never in a million years, would any of us have imagined the days leading up to the celebrating of this day! It's the first time in his fifty-nine years that Harry hasn't wished his mother a happy birthday. But he will be pleased that for a couple of hours at least, she was able to enjoy a relaxing fun birthday lunch, and that we all tried to make her feel like the special lady she is.

Our wonderful friends Dougall and Ann planned and hosted the birthday lunch for Helen today. This is only one of the *many* things they have done for our family over the last three weeks. At least one member of their family has been at the hospital every day since this all began. They have warmed our hearts with their outpouring of love for Harry, and their incredibly generous offers of help for every member of our extended family. The beautiful smiling faces of the five of them never fail to lift my spirits.

Tonight, before we left, we all stood around Harry's bed and sang "Happy Birthday" to Helen. She began to cry and when I hugged her, she said, "I'm just so happy he's made it—that he's alive" ... the best birthday gift a mother could receive ....
Cathy

"Such a great update today ... first and foremost ... A VERY HAPPY BIRTHDAY TO HARRY'S MOM!!!! She looks radiant in her picture! What wonderful friends you have to make sure your mother in law's eighty-sixth birthday was celebrated as the joyous occasion it is! You are blessed with family and friends...."
~KW

"Happy Birthday to Harry's Mom, Helen! What a beautiful lady and I see where Harry got his beautiful smile."
~GM

"What a joy to see smiling Auntie Helen on the home page this morning. I sent her card with some hesitation because I wasn't certain, in the time it would take to get there in the mail, if it would still be a 'happy' day. But, in true motherly form, she reminds us all what a tremendous gift LIFE is! Aunt Helen, we are thrilled for the gift of your life, too!"
~LH

"Cathy—the saying goes, you can't keep a good man down, and truly that is the case with your phenomenal husband. I am convinced he feels the love around him and that is what is fueling his already amazing inner strength as evident with his continued progress. I am so fortunate to talk to so many of your wonderful neighbors daily. Everyone has Harry in their prayers and hearts and we all think positive thoughts for him constantly. I must check my emails over thirty times a day but my most awaited time is every evening to get notified of your daily journal entry. Little things throughout the day prompt our thoughts of Harry. For many of us, I'm sure, it is every time we see a smile and especially those from our kids. Your strength is awe inspiring. Know that we are all with you always. All our continued thoughts and prayers."
~DW

"It is so comforting to hear first-hand of Harry's progression and healing. He has always been the one to call on birthdays, remember small details of a trip you told him about or an upcoming event. Now it will be his turn to lavish himself with all the messages that are outpouring to him and his family and to feel the love he is always so willing to give. Your family has touched so many—I hope you are able to find small comfort with these well-wishes and prayers. Sleep well and give Harry a kiss from us. :) We know we will see him soon."
~AD

"I agree with Jim C—Cathy, there are many of us out here who have learned so much from you about what to do when a loved one is in crisis. You have no doubt learned so much about what you are capable of doing. I pray that were we faced with such a crisis, we can all remain caring, kind, positive, grateful and spiritual. Perhaps that is a big "purpose" in what has happened."
~NM

"Cathy, The trials that God places before us sometimes are incomprehensible to us mere mortals. All too often, the family

bears the brunt of them as you are now. I share your love,
hope, and yes, even your underlying fears and sadness, and I
hope this boosts your strength and resolve."
~PK

Friday, August 14, 2009 Midnight

More Improvement Today!

Tonight, when I spoke with Harry's surgeon, he was pleased to let me know that Harry's kidneys are producing a lot more urine ... so much, that if this trend continues, sometime within the next week, he may be weaned from dialysis!! This is a huge step, one that was not expected this early. (And, not expected at all by some!) Normal bilirubin levels are 0.2 - 1.2. Yesterday, Harry's level was 19. Today, it is 17—one more small improvement for the day.

The feeding tube had to come out, as Harry's stomach rejected the nutrition. The undigested food sprayed everywhere, covering just about all of the IV connections and they all had to be re-done. It was quite a task! Another attempt will be made tomorrow or Sunday, this time with the tube bypassing the stomach, and going to the intestines, so that there is no risk of rejection from the stomach.

Harry's respiratory therapist took him off of the respirator for some time today, to see if Harry could still breathe on his own, and he did very well. He remained breathing comfortably for almost an hour. He was then put back on the respirator (easy to do with a tracheotomy) for his dialysis. When Harry has dialysis, he needs to remain still. The ports are in the side of his neck, and if he moves, it crimps the blood lines and the dialysis is not as successful as it would be if he were still. Even without our presence, it was a challenge for the technician to keep Harry still for the four hours of dialysis today.

Throughout the night and through most of the day, Harry was a bit agitated. He seems to be trying for a more comfortable position in the bed (and who can blame him after twenty-three days?). He's trying to swing that right leg out of bed again and push himself up on his elbows, just like 2 1/2 weeks ago. He may be trying to communicate with us through body movements, opening his eyes, and moving his head, which is what he does in response to voices and touch.

Around 4:00 p.m. today, Harry finally fell asleep. He had been busy fidgeting for almost twenty-four straight hours, so it was blessed relief to see him relax. His nurse knows that he desperately needs to sleep, so we selected soothing piano music to play from his iPod, she shut the blinds, turned down the lights, and closed the glass door to his room. She camped outside his room, and gave me the occasional thumbs-up to Harry's peacefully sleeping form.

Our friend Kenny left a letter for me at the hospital today. Once Harry fell asleep, I pulled out the letter to read, and soon I was covered in goosebumps. The gist of Kenny's letter is what I have been thinking about for days, and is what I was intending to write about tonight.

Kenny wrote, *"When my dad passed away recently, there were so many nice things said about him at his funeral, and I wish he could have heard those things while he was still alive. Once Harry recovers, it will be great for him to see how much he is loved and by how many. I'm sure he will love seeing how well his family was comforted and cared for. I can't wait to share with Harry how people came together and rallied around him and his family."*

Every night, as I read the CaringBridge guestbook entries, I am brought to tears by your outpouring of love for Harry, and your support of our family. I'm anxious to share the guestbook and personal emails and phone messages with him. So many, many times over the last weeks, I have had the same thought as Kenny—that people don't usually get to hear how much they are treasured ... because it is too late. But you are doing that for Harry, and for that—I thank you so very much!!
Cathy

"Dear Cathy and Harry,
Every day our family reads your updates and follows your progress. There isn't a day that goes by that we don't talk about you and your family and pray for your recovery. My Grandpa was admitted to the hospital after suffering a heart attack. He was also young, only in his early eighties at the time. His cardiologist was a fabulous lady—very professional, but warm and compassionate. About ten years later he was having some minor issues, so I took him in to see her. She

decided to run a stress test. Up he went on the treadmill with the wires stuck on his chest. He was walking briskly and I knew he was getting tired when his doctor said 'Now run!' Well, Grandpa looked at her, pulled the wires off, stepped off the treadmill and said, 'Are you out of your freaking mind?' After a moment of stunned silence, we all laughed so hard. So Harry ... when you are ninety-four and Harrison takes you and his mom in to see your cardiologist for a checkup, remember one thing. Ninety-four-year-olds can say anything to their doctors and get away with it, and also, that doctors love seeing the patients they saved ten years later and are still going strong. We pray for you and your family every day and can't wait for the day you come home. Your community, your loving family and friends, will celebrate your homecoming."
~CO

"I will bet good money that Harry will have quite the story to tell us. My brother had several out-of-body experiences and I think Harry will have had some, too! Love you and my heart breaks each day as we pray for our warrior to continue his journey home. PS ... My brother told us that they do wear clothes in heaven!"
~MB

"George Bernard Shaw once wrote, 'I am of the opinion that my life belongs to the community and as long as I live it, it is my privilege to do for it whatever I can.' Harry White has lived this quote with his family, his practice, on the sports fields, golf courses and baseball diamonds, and in every nook and cranny on our campus. God willing, he will continue to do so for many more years. Every place I go, I run into someone who knows Harry and his family and they react with the same dismay I had upon hearing the bad news. But the good news is that everyone seems to have a happy Harry White story! Harry, you are a man who has touched the lives of every person you have encountered with your sincere love and caring for people, your genuine interest in others, your quick smile and great hair, and your amazing ability to remember not only a name but so

much about a person you may have met for just a few passing moments. You have blessed the lives of so many people and you have certainly blessed my life. Your entire family is in my thoughts and prayers every day. Get well soon, my friend!"
~JM

"I often think about Coach White's motivational phone calls to my sons. Sometimes it's for a job well-done, sometimes it's kudos for sportsmanship and conduct. It has meant so much to them and to me, as a single parent. One of my favorite things I remember Harry saying is, 'When we all come sliding into that final home plate, we need to know that we have really lived our lives.' Dr. White—please, don't you be sliding into that final home plate any time soon!"
~JM

"So happy to hear that kidney function is improving! I would hate to think that I had seen for the last time, Harry spelling his name in the snow!"
~DB

"Harry, I was reminded yesterday of our conversation not too long ago when we discussed how much we both enjoy Alan Jackson's song 'Remember When.' When I visualize you now, it isn't of you unconscious in that hospital bed, but it's you and Cathy dancing to that song in front of your friends and family, as we celebrate your complete recovery and return to perfect health. I see you and Cathy reminiscing about the glorious lifetime you have shared and looking forward eagerly to decades more of happiness ahead in your journey together. My wife and I are comforted by the joy of these thoughts of you."
~TL

"Good Ol' Harry—Boy, you don't fool around, do you? You always seem to excel at everything and now I see you are mastering the art of survival. In your typical fashion, you have us all on the edge of our seats. What a crazy three weeks!"
~CG

"Harry—enough already! Cut the crap and get out of that place so we can go on our Wine Walk! Lord, I still cannot believe this is happening...."
~CW

"Harry is going to need that sense of humor of his when he wakes up! He's going to look down at his abdomen and ask why someone played permanent tic-tac-toe on his belly!"
~Bill S

"Cathy, My night-time routine has forever changed—play with my kids, watch ESPN, and check on Harry's daily status report. These past few days, my heart immediately fills with hope, warmth and love ... as I find myself smiling joyfully as I thank God for the miracles He is performing through Harry, and through you and Harrison. I then thank Him for all of my own blessings. Isn't that the purpose in something like this near-tragedy? What a peaceful, loving world it would be if we did this without needing a horrendous ordeal such as this to remind us."
~MF

"Oh, I am so happy to hear that Harry is still with us and continues to improve. He is such a wonderful man, and I have admired him many years as a colleague and as a friend. I am amazed that he still takes the time to send me happy birthday wishes each year. Harry has warmth and charisma that so few people have—he must be a very special husband and father. I am certain he will surprise all of the docs with his strength and will to live."
~FM

"We have our fingers, toes, arms, legs and eyes crossed in hopes of Harry's improvement. We will continue until the much-anticipated day when he walks out of that hospital! We are still on the edges of our seats each night before we open your update. We are not yet out of the woods of fear that

something might have changed throughout the day. Each day now does allow us to breathe easier, but ... well, you know how it is better than anyone."
~GW

Saturday, August 15, 2009 11:30 p.m.

Slow and Steady Progress

Today was another day of slow, steady progress. The kidneys are continuing to slightly increase their production. Although the bilirubin number is still seventeen, the other liver function numbers have improved ever so slightly. Harry had another four hour dialysis today, and was a little less agitated throughout the day.

The best news is that, for the first time in at least eight days, Harry responded this evening to the nurse's request to squeeze her hand and nod his head!! This is a big step—again, one we were not expecting this soon. Harry's improving health is a tribute to his strength and will to survive.

Harry's awesome partner, Dr. Zachary, has organized a Red Cross Blood Drive to honor Harry. Many of you told me that the hospital has enough blood, and will no longer be booking appointments. So, if you are still interested, this could be a good opportunity. Thank you, Dr. Zachary, for arranging this in honor of Harry. Nothing would please him more than a gesture like this—that so many people will benefit from what you are doing in his honor. Thank you!! XO

Looking forward to another restful, healing day tomorrow, Cathy

You are invited to a life-saving Blood Drive
In Honor of Dr. Harry L. White
Wednesday, September 2, 2009
8:30 a.m. to 7:30 p.m.
Red Cross bus will be in the parking lot

One of the many things I didn't share with anyone but the hospital staff during this week was the neurologist's concern over Harry's brain function. He wanted Harry to have an MRI done, but that isn't wise so soon after stent placement. He was very worried, though, as was I. I was still concerned about Harry surviving and now the new issue was that he might survive, but have brain damage. Eight days without response was not an encouraging turn of events. With each passing day that produced no response, brain damage was more strongly suspected. The neurologist was visibly relieved that evening, though, heaving a huge sigh of relief when he walked into the room to see for himself that Harry was finally responding!

I drove home from the hospital late that night, feeling more emotionally and physically exhausted than any other time in my life. The discouragement of the last eight days, of concern about Harry's brain function, had definitely taken its toll on me. As if the two weeks prior to that wasn't enough to handle, this new development was another serious storm to endure. Things looked better, but the stress of the past week was draining. Harrison was spending this night at his friend's house, and I knew I still had much to do when I got home, before I could slip into bed. I needed to walk the dogs, sort a load of laundry, go through the mail … the usually easy list of chores seemed huge to my exhausted soul.

When I walked in, I noticed soft light emanating from my bedroom upstairs and the dogs greeted me sleepily. There was a note at the bottom of the stairs from my mom, "The dogs have been fed and walked, the laundry has been sorted, the dishwasher emptied, and your mail is on your desk. Get some sleep! Love you, Mom."

With immense relief, I slowly trudged up the stairs, and stopped when I entered my bedroom. My mom had turned down the bed on my side, dimmed the lights low, put on soft music, left my nightgown draped across the foot of the bed, and left a note on my pillow, "Soon you will be turning down the bed on Harry's side, too!"

To this day, just thinking about my mom's sweet gesture that night brings fresh tears to my eyes. She wanted so badly to do anything she could to ease the burden of my days and this was such a perfect, tender touch of a mother's love.

I lost my mom in March of 2018 to congestive heart failure. In the five months that she was on home hospice care, I was honored to help my dad care for her. She was sharp as a tack, as her body was failing her, but that gave us many opportunities to share stories and memories and for me to tell her how much I loved her. We talked several times about the hundreds of things she and my dad did to help me while Harry was in the hospital. They always house-sat for us when we traveled, so they were familiar with the dogs' routine and with everything in the house, so it was easy for them to take over house and dog duties. It was always evident that they wanted nothing more than to help every day in any way possible. I was so thankful to have the opportunity to share my immense gratitude and love with my mom before she died. I specifically reminded my mom of what she did for me that August 15th night, and told her how much I treasured her sweetness and thoughtfulness. I learned to be compassionate, caring and giving from her and I am indeed lucky to have had the chance to tell her so.

Sunday, August 16, 2009 Midnight

A Very HAPPY Day!

Today, I saw one of the most beautiful things I have ever seen! For the first time in twenty-five days ...
HARRY SMILED!
Harry's brother, Bob, and I were standing at the end of Harry's bed, when Harry opened his eyes and seemed to focus on us. In response to our greeting, he smiled! It was a slow, weak smile, but it was definitely a smile!

For the last five days, we have kept visitors to a minimum, because of the dialysis and Harry's need to rest. With impeccable timing, for some reason today, several family members and close friends showed up at the same time. Soon after Bob and I saw Harry smile, we had ten people in the room. Harry opened his eyes and smiled many times over the next sixty minutes—and the smiles were no longer weak—they were beautiful. After each response, he would fall back asleep, but whenever he awoke, someone would greet him and he would give them a smile. It was *magical....*

Although Harry had a temperature of 103.8 through the night, his fever was down during the day. He is back on antibiotics, but cannot have Tylenol to bring down the fever, as Tylenol is metabolized in the liver. Instead, his nurse gave him cooled IV fluids to cool him down, and he was able to sleep comfortably after that. Harry's kidneys continued to produce enough urine, that he did not need dialysis today! His bilirubin and liver functions improved by small increments. As his doctor told us tonight, everything is going in the right direction.

Our dear friend, Roger, a professional musician, told me over a week ago that he had written a song for Harry. He mentioned that when Harry is ready for him to play and sing for him in his hospital room, he will be there. Several nights ago, our intensivist told me that he is supportive of anything we want to do in Harry's room to make him feel comfortable and at home. When I told him that Roger would like to play for him, he enthusiastically encouraged me to arrange it. This afternoon, Roger came to the hospital room to honor Harry with his music.

One of Harry's favorite things to do is listen to Roger play the guitar and sing. When Roger said hello to him tonight, Harry smiled, but he opened his eyes wide and smiled again when Roger told him that his beautiful wife, Diane, was there, too! Kevin,  Roger and Diane's son, and Harrison gathered with us around the bed, and watched Harry relax as Roger sang. It's a moment I will never forget. When Roger sang the song he wrote for Harry, I don't think there was a dry eye in the room. The song is called ...

"Harry's Smile"

Goodnight!

Cathy

In a moment, In a lifetime,
How you never even know
In a blink, it can take you
to a place you've never gone
When you think you got it made,
It'll drop you to your knees, I'm
here to tell you, life is better
on the days that
Harry Smiles
Someone told me, that the test of
a friend would feel this way
We'll all be better

When he's back again I have to say
Something about him, you just can't deny
Here to tell you, life was better in the time when
Harry Smiles
Oh take my hand and comfort me
Oh dry your eyes and you will see
Sure things will be different now
We're gonna make it through somehow
All the family and the lives you touch
All the love you share that means so much
You make the world a better place, ain't no doubt
My life will never be the same
'cause I been touched by
Harry's Smile.

"We can never know all the good that a simple smile can do."
~Mother Teresa

"Today was an unforgettable joy for my wife and me. To see you smile at the two of us when we stood next to you at your bedside brought huge crocodile tears of relief to our eyes and happiness to our hearts. What a breakthrough! Just the simple things, watching you move your shoulder and later your leg, consciously trying to achieve a more comfortable position in your bed, well ... It was exhilarating! And then to be fortunate enough to share these moments with your mom and dad, brother Bob, Cathy, Harrison, and a handful of close friends, was an experience that was just off the charts! For us, this is proof positive that miracles do happen!"
~TL

"Your latest journal entry gave me thrill-bumps and I thought of two things immediately. Harry is communicating his joy of having friends and loved ones around him, and he is giving all of you the gift of his smile to let you know everything is going to be OK. It is yet another example of his selfless desire to spread sunshine and happiness!

Congratulations on such an enormous milestone—this is one worth celebrating indeed!"
~CG

"What a delight it was to read your Sunday evening journal. When I read that Harry smiled at you and other members of your family, I sighed with the greatest relief and thought, 'oh, thank you God.' I can only imagine the unfettered joy that is filling your heart, knowing that Harry is experiencing an increased level of awareness and has the ability to convey this to you. Hopefully, each day will bring additional blessings as he continues on the road to full recovery. He is so loved by everyone who knows him, we all want him back with you and Harrison as soon as it is Heavenly possible. Thank you so very much for sharing his courageous journey with us. God bless you always."
~MK

"Dr. White, I wanted to let you know that my entire family and my youth group are praying for you to get better. You have made a great impact on my life through football and just every time I see you. You always ask me how I am and show a genuine interest in me. You also encourage me in whatever I'm doing and I'm thankful for your kindness and compassion. I know that God is going to heal you. I know He is in control. Mrs. White and Harrison, you are in my thoughts and prayers also and I hope that you are being comforted by friends and family. Please let us know if there's anything our family can do. Get better soon so I can see your smile around campus again."
~LW

"This has been the hardest story to believe. My husband just saw you, Harry, walking into the racquet club the night before all this happened. When he came home from the club the next day, he told me the news and we just couldn't believe it was true. Harry, if there was ever someone in life who truly looks to make a positive difference in other people's lives, it is you. It is very evident that God has very special plans for you here

on this earth and that you're so faithful to His calling. I know He has you in His precious hands holding you ever so tenderly as you go through this painful ordeal. He's given a reminder to all of us how precious life really is and how quickly we can be taken out of our comfort zones. I believe we all cherish our loved ones even more because of what you've been through. That's God still working through your pain. Cathy, I admire the courage and strength you display as you deal with each day ... the good and the bad. God is using you as well to show us the peace He gives to those who place their trust in Him. Harrison, you have a great mom and dad. Your dad has been constantly covered with so many prayers, from so many people, who love and care about him. God is listening and hears all those prayers. It may take a while, but your dad will be back home with you again, doing all the fun things you're used to doing together. Hang in there! He is so proud of you."
~EN

"I did not need to hear the song about Harry's smile to bring tears to my own eyes. Harry's smile is unforgettable and even during the critical days, I could still see and feel him smiling. Last night, our son brought out the letters that you both wrote to him when Harry was his baseball coach. You told him how impressed you were with his concern for others and how polite he was, always greeting you and asking about your son. You will never know how much those letters meant and still mean to him. The fact that you took the time to write them and to make a difference in his life is something remarkable. He cherishes those letters and will never forget you for caring enough. That is what I will always remember too-that you care enough! Both of you have servants' hearts towards your community, family and friends. No matter what the venue, you are taking care of everyone and not because you have to, but because you want to. We love you guys for all that you've done to enrich our lives. We welcome the opportunity to give back to you with the same love and consideration as you've clearly given. God bless you all and Godspeed in your recovery, Harry!"
~JH

"A smile costs nothing but gives much. It enriches those who receive without making poorer those who give. It takes but a moment, but the memory of it sometimes lasts forever. None is so rich or mighty that he cannot get along without it and none is so poor that he cannot be made rich by it. Yet a smile cannot be bought, begged, borrowed, or stolen, for it is something that is of no value to anyone until it is given away. Some people are too tired to give you a smile. Give them one of yours, as none needs a smile so much as he who has no more to give."
~Author Unknown

Monday, August 17, 2009 - Midnight

Harry's Wall of Fame

Harry was taken off the ventilator all day today—he is breathing very well on his own. He will go back on it for the night, so that he can breathe without setting off alarms which wake him up. Tomorrow—he will be back on his own, and we shall see what happens from there. Harry received dialysis today for three hours, but his kidney output continues to increase by the day, so no dialysis is expected for tomorrow. Liver functions are improving slightly again today.

I got a few more smiles today, though weaker than yesterday. When the nurse asked Harry if he was in pain, he slowly shook his head yes. When she told him that she had some medication for him he said, "Okay ... yes," —the first words to the staff in weeks. A physical therapist came by to work with him while I was there, but Harry was sleepy, so the session was used more to test his flexibility and range of motion, which looked remarkably good for spending twenty-six days in bed.

Just a reminder—Harry's visitor situation is very limited. He cannot have visitors during dialysis, which is a three to five hour process. The dialysis ports are in the jugular vein in his neck. If he moves, the blood line gets crimped and the process is not as successful as it is when he is still. We are also trying to establish a consistent sleep schedule for him. What he needs most right now is rest. Harry will be hospitalized for many more weeks, and there will come a time when visits are more appropriate. Please be patient. Dozens of people have asked me if they can visit, and eventually the answer will be yes, but now is not the best time. Always call me before you intend to visit, because if I haven't left your name at the CCU desk, you won't be able to get in.

Today was the start of football "hell week" for Harrison. He has practice twice a day—from 8-11:30 a.m. and from 4-7:30 p.m. Between practices today, the senior players 'initiated' the freshmen by buzzing their hair. Harrison's new 'do' is in the shape of an H (his nickname is H-Man), and his number 3 is etched in the hair on the side of his head. In Harry's pain-killer, sedative induced state, he may have trouble recognizing his own son!

Last night, after Harry's intensivist finished examining him, he spent some time looking at Harry's "Wall of Fame", the pictures and quotes that are in the room. He took the time to read everything, and then turned to the nurse and said, "Wow! This man is very well loved. The world needs more people like this. We need to do everything we can to get him back to his family and community as quickly as we can."

Until tomorrow,
Cathy

"Since I first got the news about Harry three weeks ago, he has been in my thoughts each and every hour! When I think of him, I ask God to be with him, and to keep him strong. I also pray for Cathy and H-Man, because we can only imagine how tough this has been on them. I really don't know Harry very well, but I did spend an afternoon with him one sunny day in his backyard. We sipped on a couple of beers and talked about children and love of family. I knew in my heart that day that 'This is a very good man.' I believe God knows that we need him here and that is why He did not take him from us. Too many people, in addition to his family, love him too much to let him go. Thank you, God, for returning Harry to us. When you get him again, it will be a glorious day in Heaven, but please ... Not for a long, long time, okay?"
~MF

"I am so happy to read of Harry's progress, especially THIS! Harry has been one of my heroes that I have admired since I was a little kid and I know now that he will recover just fine. He is Superman and nothing bad happens to Superman ... or his perfect hair."
~NG

"I am thrilled that it looks like I can now look forward to seeing your Dentine smile and Breck-perfect hair again

someday. Keep getting stronger, Harry—you have countless friends praying for just that!"
~CG

"Every morning when I get up, I let the dog out, turn on the coffee pot, and then go straight to my computer to read about the daily miracles that Cathy has so beautifully shared with all of us. I know that it is just a matter of time before Dr. White comes bouncing back into the office with his abundance of positive energy and that beautiful smile, saying hello to everyone and asking us all how we are doing. I have never witnessed such an outpouring of love and support as I have on this website and it is all so well-deserved for a man who has given so much to his community, patients, friends and family. Dr. White, you are always in my prayers and thoughts. Cathy, you are one amazing woman. A truly great role model for all of us.
With all my heart,"
~GB

"Oh girl, we have been waiting so long for that smile! From the first time I saw that smile and met you both in 1979, smiling is what we do best. So many people owe their smiles to Harry, including me! (And at fifty-six, I still wear my retainer!) We have shared so much through the years and can't wait to share many more wonderful memories. All I can say is, 'Thank God!!!'"
~JH

Tuesday, August 18, 2009 11:53 p.m.

What a Difference a Day Makes

Every morning, I call Harry's day nurse at 9:00 to check on him and to see what procedures are scheduled for the day. I wait until shift change is accomplished between 7:00 and 8:00, then give her some time to evaluate Harry's condition. He had two nurses today, the same two as yesterday. When I asked Dede how Harry was doing today, there was a pause ... and my stomach dropped. Then she said, "Oh my gosh, Cathy! Harry is doing great! You won't believe the difference between yesterday and today. I've seen a lot as a nurse, and I am amazed." ... I told her I was on my way!!!

When my dear friend, Batzi, and I walked into the room, Harry was sitting up in bed, and turned to look at us and smiled. We talked with him off and on for almost two hours. He can't speak with the tracheotomy tube in, because no air passes through his vocal cords, so for a while, we did some lip reading. Then, the nurse put a special valve on the trach opening, which allowed him to speak, although very softly, and sometimes with difficulty in understanding on our part. He would drift off to sleep between conversations, then awaken and smile at us again.

A physical therapist helped get Harry out of bed today!! He was able to sit at the edge of the bed, then stand (with assistance), and even shuffled a couple of side steps. He was aware enough to follow all the requests of the therapist, who was greatly pleased, and also remarked on the vast difference between yesterday and today.

No dialysis was done today, and the liver numbers are all still improving. Harry was off the ventilator all day. The feeding tube went back in, and this time, Harry's system tolerated it. Tomorrow morning, he will have a swallowing evaluation, and if he passes that, he will be able to start drinking small amounts of water.

When the nurse asked Harry if he was ready for more pain medication, he said, "Yes, please." Every time someone finished doing something for him, he said, "Thank you." He asked where Harrison was. Harry mentioned Batzi's dog to her, and asked about our dogs. He responded to her so well, even giving a weak, little laugh here and there. When she told him that she loved him, he said, "I love you, too, Batzi."

Batzi told Harry that his mom had been to see him every day, and she said she thought that it was so sweet. He shook his head yes and said, "Sweet." At least twenty times, he said he wanted to go home!! He said he wanted to go sleep at home. He asked where he was and looked confused when I told him that he was in the hospital. He didn't ask anything beyond that, about what had happened, or how long he has been in the hospital. Later, he said, "This is a very different environment." HA, different indeed!!!

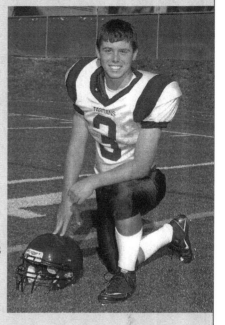

I took down the photo of the football team from the wall and held it in front of Harry. I told him that they took it just for him, and he said, "Wow! Cool. There's H-Man!"

Harry had a very busy day. He got out of bed and stood on his feet for the first time in twenty-seven days, and had a little workout. He was occasionally alert, talked quite a bit, and had his first portion of digestible nutrition in almost a month. He was very ready for a good night's sleep. Before leaving tonight, I said, "I'm going to go pick up Harrison from football practice, and I'll see you tomorrow. Goodnight, Harry. I love you!" He turned to me and mouthed, "I love you, too, Cat."

Ahhhhh ... what a difference a day makes!
Cathy

"Reading your update today brought me tears of joy. I am elated to hear of Harry's progress. I think we are all

*beginning to no longer fear another setback!! Yay! Yes, what
a difference a day makes! I know Harry will be fine—he
is strong and has a heart of gold. His survival is not only a
miracle, but I think it is a special gift from God—a reward to
Harry for all the good he has done for other people. Thinking
of you all with much love.... "*
~MF

*"These days, as difficult as they are, truly bring out the
good in people. Trying times have a way of showing us what
people are made of. You've always been that shining light
for us, in our darkest hours, Harry. I have no idea how we
would've come this far, after losing our son, without the love
and support of you, Cathy and Harrison. There were moments
when we didn't know how to catch our breath, moments when
we didn't know how to move forward to the next moment, they
were that bad. I think that God puts people in our lives to help
prop us up, when we are unable to stand on our own. To me,
the truest, most pure form of love is what you can do for those
who cannot do for themselves. We all switch roles in that act,
in our lifetimes. I'm so grateful for our friendship...."*
Love, Batzi

*"Yay Harry! You are on your way back to us! Smiles, off the
ventilator all day, a few words, all are beautiful music to our
ears. I can't wait to hear Cathy tell us, "Harry was dancing in
the halls today." I am so sorry that you've had to go through
this but if you ever wondered how much you're loved you
now know! Can you believe this beautiful journal? What a
wonderful gift it will be for you.
All our love,"*
~CR

*"Harry ... You've stepped up to the plate. The tying run is on
second and you are the winning run at the plate. No matter
what the pitcher throws at you, you just keep fouling them
off! You know what the stats in baseball say.... The batter is
always favored to win this battle. So, way to battle! Now let's*

106

*see that home run! ... And the crowd goes wild ... Woo hoo ...
Harry is our hero and Team White is victorious!"*
~JH

*"Sister Cathy - Gorgeous Harry is so strong and brave. I bet you
admire him and have fallen in love with him even more these
past few weeks. I am praying for you both, for Harrison, for
your families and for all of us who love you so. Harry has never
missed a birthday call to me in over thirty years. I expect one
this year. Tell him heavy breathing will do.... I love you,"*
~Sister C

*"We were just getting ready to write something here when
we happened to glance at the visitor number at the top of
the screen—you've had 4997 visits from family and friends
... that's amazing! You're obviously loved so much by so
many—and it's not hard to see that we're not the only ones
who consider you and Harry two of the greatest people we
know. We have the best of times when we're with you—and
we always look forward to the next time—and now we can't
wait to see your and Harry's smiling faces again. It is such a
relief to know that Harry is slowly but surely recovering, and
although the road of healing will most likely be a long one, at
least he'll be taking that road.... We're still amazed at your
strength and uplifting attitude, Cathy, we've said it before, but
you are one strong, resilient, beautiful person. We've been
thinking about your family every day and still can't go to sleep
without checking your latest update for Harry's status."*
~LN

*"Oh, to hear Harry say he loves you—oh my, how great was
that?!!!! When my husband was reading this to me last night
I just couldn't believe it and now that I am sitting here this
morning and re-reading it, I am brought to tears. Let me shout
out in my loudest NY voice—AMEN!!! We are absolutely
thrilled for your family. Here's to the power of prayer and
most of all LOVE!!!!"*
~LK

Wednesday, August 19, 2009 Midnight

Day 28

Can you believe it? Twenty-eight days of hospitalization? Four weeks ago tonight, life was so normal, so peaceful and enjoyable. Little did we know how much our lives were about to change!

Every morning, Harry's blood results determine what he needs for the day. His BUN and creatinine (kidney function) were a bit high today, so he had dialysis for three hours. Unfortunately, high BUN and creatinine levels can also cause nausea. Yep, you guessed it—Harry tossed his cookies ... *all over himself.* EVERYTHING needed to be replaced—every IV, every monitor, every catheter, every dressing, even the abdominal dressing. So much for a peaceful day!

Once Harry finished dialysis, got all 'new equipment' and got cleaned up, he actually did have a peaceful day. He is still very out of it, because of his pain meds. But he is calm and responsive, and once woken up, smiles and tries to talk. If the valve is in, we can hear his softly spoken words, otherwise, we make a valiant effort to lip read. When we asked him what he thought of Harrison's buzz cut, he said, "Love it!" He laughs and responds well to humor. He looks very quizzically at all of the odd things attached to him, and sometimes asks about them. With each passing day, he will comprehend and remember more, and soon conversations will be more normal. For now, talking is very sweet in its simplicity. When I left tonight, I bent to kiss his cheek, and he turned to me and puckered up for a kiss. SO sweet!!!!

Good-night,
Cathy

In the first week or so of Harry regaining consciousness, he never slipped back into a medication-induced coma, but he wasn't very lucid or focused either. It wasn't like waking up from sleep—a minute or two to awaken, then normal interaction. Harry was still so heavily affected by sedation, pain medication and his lack of organ function from

Abdominal Compartment Syndrome, that most of the time, especially in the first few days, I considered him to be very "out-of-it," even when his eyes were open and he was trying to speak. Dozens of times per day, he would look around exhaustedly, then drift off to sleep. Then, he would awaken, say something fairly lucid, then drop back to sleep as if the effort to talk were too great for him. Sometimes his eyes would flutter shut while he was trying to talk. He was no longer unconscious, but he was very far from normal memory and communication. He was still so out-of-it that he hadn't even yet asked what happened. He knew he was in the hospital, but hadn't asked any other questions.

This evening, Wednesday, I decided to go back to see him at the hospital, just for an hour or so, after Harrison and I had dinner. I left Harrison at home, but when I told Batzi that I was just going for a quick visit, she said she wanted to go with me. We had talked over a dozen times about this topic, but we wondered aloud if Harry "saw the light." Harry was still days, probably more like weeks away, from having a lucid conversation about anything, so until then, we enjoyed speculating on our quick drive to the hospital.

Harry was especially sleepy that night, but we had a peaceful, quiet visit in his dimly lit room. Batzi and I stood on either side of the bed, talking softly to each other. About every ten minutes, Harry would sleepily open his eyes, look at us both, smile, squeeze our hands, then go back to sleep. We had been standing there for about an hour and were preparing to leave, so that Harry could get some rest without trying to awaken for us.

Suddenly, Harry opened his eyes, which were clear and focused, like they hadn't been in four weeks. He looked at me intently, holding my gaze and said, "I was out of my body." I said, "You were? Are you talking about the night your heart stopped?" He said, in disbelief, "Yes—how did you know that?" I told him that I was there and asked if he saw me. He concentrated on the question, then said that no, he hadn't seen me. He held my gaze steadily again and whispered, "I flat-lined." I said, "Yes, you most certainly did. Did you see the white light?" Again, he concentrated on the answer and replied, "It was behind me and it was very warm."

I glanced at Batzi, who was crying by now. She said, "Harry, were you afraid?" Harry turned to her, clearly understanding why she was

109

asking that question. Batzi had lost one of her sons, Chase, to a car accident less than three years prior. With complete understanding and compassion, Harry said, "Oh, no, Batzi! I wasn't afraid at all. It was wonderful. I'm sure Chase wasn't afraid. Don't worry. Chase was never afraid." Batzi said, "You came back. Did someone ask you if you wanted to go back or stay there?" He concentrated again and haltingly he said, "Yes. Someone asked me if I wanted to go back—it was a deep, loving voice ... and I said, "Yes, I want to go back." It wasn't easy to say yes— it was so beautiful there." He looked thoughtful again, and said in quiet amazement, "I was above my body, looking down at the monitors. The line was flat and there was a really loud alarm." Batzi and I were holding his hands, telling him how happy we were that he decided to come back to us, when he fell back into a peaceful sleep.

It was at least a month before we would again talk about this out-of-body experience. After Harry was home and had regained some strength and stamina, his brain got better at processing information and remembering things. When he did bring up being above his body, the scenario was exactly the same as what he told us that night in the hospital.

Over the next several days, Harry would repeatedly tell Batzi and me about a young boy that worried him. He asked if we could get the poor thing some ice cream, because he was so sad. When we asked why he was sad, he said that he was sad about the fourteen-year-old girl— that she was all alone, because everyone on the airplane died. He must have repeated this story and his concern at least a dozen times over the next four to five days. He mentioned that the boy was around twelve, maybe from India, with beautiful skin and eyes, that he had stood in the corner, over by the drapes when he was talking to Harry. Initially, I thought these were ramblings from his drug-induced brain. Harry was so sure of himself when he spoke of this boy, and he was so bothered by the boy's grief, that I began to wonder if there was something genuine here. After hearing about his being above his body, I knew anything was possible and I also considered that Harry might have died and come back more than once. I asked Batzi to look into this for me and what she found shook us both to the core. In June of 2009, there had been a plane crash in the Indian Ocean and the only survivor of a large family was ... a 14-year-old girl.

We can't explain what was happening here, but it is an indication to me that there is so much that exists beyond the realm of our understanding here on earth. Was Harry in "limbo," communicating with this young boy who perished in the crash? Maybe. We will never know exactly what transpired, but it has certainly opened our eyes to the possibilities.

Thursday, August 20, 2009 Well Past Midnight

Another Good Day

I'll keep this brief tonight, as it is late and I have just returned from the hospital. Whew! A long day, but a very good one.

Harry didn't need dialysis or the respirator. His bilirubin is down, and his skin is less yellow. His kidney output continues to improve. He got out of bed again today, and with the help of two physical therapists on each side, he shuffled to a chair, where he sat for an hour. While he was in the chair, he did some exercises with his legs and arms. He also had his swallow evaluation for liquids and passed. He has been having ice chips all day. Such a simple thing, but one that has made him very happy!

The biggest improvement today was in Harry's communication with us. He is getting very comfortable talking with the valve in place. So, chatting with him today was productive and fun! He is still under the influence of medications, so sometimes he says things that confuse us. But sometimes he surprises us with the lucidity and depth of his thoughts. And, he certainly hasn't lost his sense of humor!

Over the last few days, Harry has spent a lot of time gazing curiously at everything attached to his body, and at every monitor and IV bag. I knew it was only a matter of time before he said, "What the heck?..." Sure enough, today he asked ... what happened to him.

I kept it simple, letting him know that he has been very sick, that there have been complications, that he has been in the hospital, that he is now improving greatly. I didn't yet tell him how many days he has been hospitalized. He remembered that he went into the hospital on Thursday morning, and was supposed to get out on Saturday—but he didn't remember the heart issues or the ambulance. We explained that his kidneys had failed, which is why he needed dialysis. He pointed to his stomach, and I explained that he had to have surgery. Later in the day, we explained to him that the abdomen was still open, and he actually watched when the wound evacuation system was changed. He said, "It doesn't look bad at all." :-)

Looking forward to another good day tomorrow,
Cathy

*"I stopped by to see Harry this morning prior to his dialysis.
He is looking good! He kept pointing straight ahead to
the photo of you, Harrison and himself, as if to say he has
somewhere to go. He does—HOME!!!"*
~SG

*"My heart is filled with joy at reading about Harry today.
I thank God for his progress and friendship. This miracle
reminds me that God is as close as a whisper. Thank you, my
Heavenly Father, for taking care of Harry and his family."*
~DR

*"We are so elated to hear the wonderful news about Harry's
recovery and survival! For me, the feeling was like I had
an eight-ounce espresso in five minutes with a king-sized
Snickers bar!! Harry, there is a saying that goes, 'You can't
keep a good man down.' But in your case, it should be, 'Clear
the pathway, a great man coming through!' Please hurry down
the path to wellness with great pace."*
~MM

*"We are thrilled to read that Harry is on his feet and talking.
That just didn't seem possible two weeks ago, but obviously
Harry is very strong and the prayers for him are working.
Please tell him that we love him and can't wait to see him
again with his warm smile, wonderful sense of humor and the
perfect hair!"*
~SD

*"I was just about to go to bed ... it is past midnight ... but
decided instead to turn on the computer and I am so glad I
did! I love the happy news that has been coming through!
Harry has been through so much and his progress has been
slow. Never in a million years did we expect him to be sitting*

up and interacting as he is now. What a huge leap! We are so encouraged, hopeful and thankful that Harry is miraculously beating the odds. That light is getting brighter at the end of the tunnel, Cathy. We are happy that after so many days of waiting, you are receiving this wonderful gift!
We love you all,"
~P and K

"What wonderful news is coming through these days!! I jumped up and did a little happy dance! I was joyfully stunned when you wrote that they had him up out of bed, as he still has one surgery to go on his abdomen, yes? My, my, Harry, you are a fighter, and we thank God for that! God is good, and I've never doubted that, but this just makes me want to shout it out, 'GOD IS GOOD!!' What a blessing to hear what a wonderful day it was ... I will mark this date on my calendar as a day to remember."
~LH

Friday, August 21, 2009 11:26 p.m.

A Restful Day with More Improvement

Harry enjoyed a restful day. This morning, a new dialysis catheter was put in, just before his three-hour dialysis treatment. The catheter that was removed a couple of days ago is believed to be the source of his recent fever, as cultures from it were positive. The liver numbers have all improved. Bilirubin went from fourteen yesterday to seven today!! Full kidney function is—almost there! As Harry drifted in and out of sleep, he was even able to enjoy some of the Little League World Series on television.

After yesterday's brief explanation of what happened to him, Harry today talked quite a bit about the day he went into the hospital. Some things, he remembers well. He remembers that it was a Thursday morning, and that he was supposed to get out of the hospital on Saturday. He recalls the pain while lying in bed, early that Thursday morning, and remembers me calling 911. Other details are very fuzzy and some of what he says makes no sense, but that's what drugs will do to your brain!!! In a more lucid moment, he said to me, "You must have been scared." (I didn't tell him that I wasn't really afraid during that first day, but that I was *very* afraid many times after that!) I said, "I'm just happy that you are okay," to which he replied, "I'm not okay yet ... but I will be."

Since Harry has begun to respond, he has been so kind and polite to everyone who works with him, or visits him. We aren't surprised by this, are we? He has a wonderful Patient Care Assistant named Alex, and whenever Alex helps him, Harry will give him the thumbs up and say, "Thanks, buddy, we're in this together." His attitude is strong and positive. His sense of humor is refreshing. Every nurse, doctor, assistant and therapist leaves his room with a smile. Even in his extremely compromised state, Harry is the man we know and love—making that positive connection with everyone with whom he comes in contact.

Happy Weekend,
The Whites

"SAAATU ! ... (Amen in Buddhism) This is it, this is the moment we've been praying for. It has finally arrived. Harry has again made us all happy. Soon, you'll see Harry's face when he reads this labouring of love you've been keeping up nightly. Thank you, Cathy, for providing us with the journal and such wonderful news across the world. We'll keep our morning and night prayers going ... that he'll be resting at home as he wishes sooner than we expect. Prayers from Thailand,"
~SK

"I sit here typing with tears still in my eyes from reading about Harry's progress. It is so great that he is up and communicating with you. You know the way he loves to talk and with twenty-nine days of not talking he has a lot of catching up to do !!!!"
~LF

"I have grown to know a Harry I never knew. Everyone knows him in their own special way and how he makes us feel, which is an incredible gift. You are so lucky to have such a treasure in your life and he is equally lucky to have such a very special person in his life. Thank you so very much for your candid commentary on Harry's journey. Love to you, Harry and Harrison,"
~JD

"I am another one of those who has been brought to tears when reading about the amazing steps to recovery that Harry had made. In my mind, I am picturing Harry's progress like he is now standing on first base after a long battle at the plate. Now, with his "heavy hitter" teammates (family/doctors/ nurses) coming up to bat, and all the fans (friends) cheering in the stands, it won't be long before we see him stealing second, rounding third, and heading for home!! Go, Harry, Go!!"
~GS

Saturday, August 22, 2009 11:57 p.m.

Working Toward a Goal ...

This morning, Harry started his day with physical therapy, and did very well. He had three hours of dialysis this afternoon. His kidney output is the best today since his kidneys first failed, so we are getting closer and closer to full function. Blood test results on kidney and liver functions continue to inch toward "within normal limits." Most of the massive swelling has left his body, and he is looking so much like himself now, albeit many pounds lighter.

Harry is still loopy at times. He occasionally says things that are humorous in their inaccuracies and expectations, and it is everything I can do to keep a straight face. But, sometimes, he is so sharp and lucid. Tonight, he was telling us all about his internal organs and what needs to happen before he goes home. I was shocked at how organized his thoughts were, and how he had remembered and understood things told to him over just the last two days.

Earlier in the day, while he watched the Angels game on TV, I told him that Mark Buehrle had pitched a perfect game on the day that Harry was admitted to the hospital. He immediately gave me all the correct criteria for a perfect game, and talked about how rare it is. But, then five minutes later, he asked what car he brought to the hospital—did he drive the black car? I told him that he came in an ambulance, and asked if he remembered the ride—either ride to either hospital, and he said he didn't.

Harry is very determined to get out of the hospital. He wants to work hard at his physical therapy, and says he will be ready for the 'sixty and over marathon' in a month! Long after the physical therapists left his room today, he was doing exercises while in bed. When we all spoke with the surgeon today, Harry told him that he really wants to be out of the hospital to see his son's first football game on September 5th. The doctor told him that it *might* be a possibility, but there is much to be done before then. Harry is driven by his goal to see that football game. If anybody can do it, Harry can! (He also told the doctor that the best way for him to recover would be to go home for a while—to hang out by the pool, sit in the jacuzzi, drink a margarita, then come back to the hospital!) :-)) Especially funny when you consider that we don't have a pool or jacuzzi, and Harry doesn't particularly care for margaritas!

Harrison made it through the first week of two-a-day practices, and had a 3 1/2 hour practice this morning. Next week is the same schedule—two practices per day, Monday through Friday, and one on Saturday. Although he played flag football for four years, this past Thursday was the first time he played in pads ... and he *loved* it! He says his dad is his inspiration—that no matter how tough football might get—it doesn't compare to what his dad has gone through. He's following the advice of his friend who said, "Do what your dad would want you to do."

Tonight, Harry asked Harrison to lie on the bed next to him. Very delicately, he did so, and Harry rubbed H's buzz cut while he told him how proud he was of him. They looked at the picture on the wall of Harrison in his Tartans football uniform. I had told Harry earlier in the day how proud *I* was of Harrison—of how he has handled himself through this horrendous ordeal, of his commitment to football, of what a source of strength and comfort he has been for me, how he offers to help me around the house, about the eight-page letter he wrote for his dad on the day of the heart issue, and how he sleeps every night with Harry's tee shirt next to him—the t-shirt that Harry was wearing the morning that he was taken to the hospital.

Tonight, when we left, Harry smiled at us and waved, and I felt the best that I have felt in 31 days!
Cathy

"Harry, The picture of you and the 'H-man' together in your hospital bed is so dear! Brought tears, as my prayers these past weeks so often have been about a young teenage boy needing a dad—a loving, active, involved dad that you have been and are—and that alone is reason enough that 'now is NOT your time' to go, so to speak. Not that Cathy doesn't need and want you around for another forty just as much (of course!!), but the photo is so precious. Your will, your fight, your strength, your faith, and that of your wonderful family and friends, has been a very powerful testimony to a great many."
~PN

"That's the Harry White I know! Positive, no matter what. I can just see him looking down at his wound and saying, like the Black Knight in Monty Python whose torso was missing, 'Just a scratch, really!'"
~KW

"I now know why I cry every day when I read the updates. I think of you as another brother. So it hurts to hear Cathy say you watched as your wound was evacuated. I am so thankful for another day of progress. This has been a long haul for you but bright days are to come. You are experiencing the Sun rise upon you. God says, "Not today Harry . . . there is so much more work to be done." I never knew the depth I felt for you until this happened. Thank you for every kind thought, every heavenly e-mail, and letting me enter into such a kind family. Cathy is the special one woman for you and you are lucky to have found that perfect match."
~DR

*"Dearest Cathy and Harry,
You touched our family when we first met over thirty years ago while you were walking Peanut Butter and Jelly one day. The obvious love you shared with each other and everyone around you always shined through both your brilliant smiles. Hearing and reading about Harry's illness was and continues*

to be heartbreaking. Cathy, reading your daily journal has been an incredible inspiration of strength, love and faith. Your continued love story brings a warm smile to my heart. I am thrilled to hear the good news of Harry's progress. Abundant thoughts and prayers are with you and all your loved ones. Warm Regards,"
~SD

"I have read your journals every day. I have cried, smiled, and often laughed out loud at your comments! I am so happy that Harry is improving but certainly not surprised considering his strong desire to get back home with his loving family again and of course to see H-man play his first football game of the season. Cathy, your courage, strength and compassion, not to mention sense of humor throughout all this, is an inspiration to all of us, and Harry, you keep getting better and keep smiling as you are missed by all of us!!! My love and prayers go out to each of you every day!"
~KL

"Dearest Cathy,
How wonderful it was to see the picture of Harry with Harrison in his hospital bed. He looks soooo good, knowing, by your diligent updates, how drastically different he looked only a few weeks ago. I'm just so thrilled to see him, even if it is only a picture. Every night I log onto my computer to get the update on how he's doing and the news from the last few days has been wonderfully encouraging. Such an answer to our prayers ... simply amazing.... (I guess that's how miracles are and Harry is truly a living miracle.) I think I might burst from the joy I feel in my soul. I'm incredibly happy that he is doing so well. Harry will remain a priority in our prayers and I look forward to his continued progress until he's 100 percent and you can bring him home. Oh, what a happy day that will be. :)"
~DS

Sunday, August 23, 2009 Midnight

A Move to a New Room

Harry was doing so well today, that he was moved to a new room tonight! His liver numbers are very slightly better, but his kidney numbers are the best they have been in the thirteen days we have been at this hospital. His bladder catheter was removed today—a huge step! Physical therapy today saw him walking (assisted) across the room, sitting in a chair, and doing lots of exercises. His breathing is strong, needing no assistance from the respirator.

Now that Harry is awake and aware for many hours of the day, it is extremely important for him to sleep well through the night. CCU is the worst place to get a good night's sleep. Not their fault—just what they need to do for the benefit of their patients. Every hour, he is awakened with necessary tests and procedures. There is light, noise and sleep disruption. These have all been essential in the past weeks for his survival, but now that he isn't under sedation, and now that his condition is not so serious, it's time to focus on rest, healing, exercise and nutrition.

Harry was moved to sub-ICU shortly before 8:00 tonight, and is looking forward to his first night of sleep in a quiet, dark environment in thirty-two days. (Can you imagine being around light, noise, and procedures every hour for 768 straight hours?!?!) When I left him tonight, he was enjoying his new digs, was being well cared-for and was ready to settle down for some much-appreciated rest.

I cannot say enough nice things about our experience here. Tonight, when we left CCU, everyone wished us well, gave us hugs, and told us they were sad to see us go. The nurses, doctors, assistants and many various therapists—have all treated us like family. They have been extremely professional, but compassionate, warm and communicative. We are on a different floor of the hospital, with different staff members, but the feeling is the same—we are still being treated like family.

Good-night,
Cathy

"I'd put my money on you being out of the hospital to see H-Man's first football game. Yes, getting out of the hospital would be good for you. But let's be truthful ... once you leave you won't be back! We are so proud of your determination and strength. Keep up the great work, friend. We know it's hard, but it will get your rear out of the hospital faster."
~SB

"It is so good to hear he has made such improvement in recent days. Believe me, I know how significant it is. I have cared for many patients, over many years; and his progress is a miracle in so many ways. Family, friends—their prayers and thoughts—add so much to recovery and a laugh or two also helps. I'm glad he has a sense of humor ... it means he is gaining a sense of well-being, a real positive. Please tell him, he is in our family's prayers."
~MD

"Harry, your new nickname will be the Miracle Man. THE WORLD IS A BETTER PLACE NOW THAT YOU ARE BACK."
~DW

"Harry and Cathy, It was great getting back to this site after my vacation and seeing the fabulous improvement. I really hope this return to greatness continues even if you have gotten significantly older during your hospitalization, which has been just about as long as your working career was!!! (I—we—am just envious). Now, maybe the rest of us can keep up with you. Can we just do golf when you fully return and finally have the time to answer all your fabulous friends and thank them for their undying (now that is a word that fits) support, which must have played a very important part in your recovery. Also, when you told your doc about the need for a Margarita, jacuz and pool—hurry up so we can all join you! Sounds like a great goal to set. Love and continue to get back to better than before,"
~BN

"I keep thinking about how AMAZING it will be for Harry to again sleep at home in his very own bed! We think of you all every day and we always thank you, Cathy, for these updates. We would be going CRAZY wondering, if you weren't doing this for us!
Love you,"
~NE

Monday, August 24, 2009 Midnight

Some Decent Sleep!

Harry got his first decent night of sleep last night for the first time in a very long time. He probably slept four to five hours straight—a far cry from the thirty-one nights before that. He is thrilled with his new environment! He had dialysis today, but his kidney function numbers are improving. The liver numbers are about the same. Harry continues to breathe on his own, and we can expect the tracheotomy tube to be removed after the surgeries are done to close his abdomen. The first phase of closing will most likely be Friday. It will probably take two to three surgeries to complete the closing. (For those of you wondering how Harry does physical therapy, etc., with his abdomen open—there is a dressing and taping all around it, and a wrap around his body that supports him and holds him in relative comfort. He evens adjusts his position easily in bed and in a chair with the support of this wonderful bit of apparel!)

The dialysis technician asked me today how many days we had been at the other hospital before arriving here. I looked down at Harry and asked him if he knew how long it had been. When he said no, I told him it was nineteen days, and that today was day fourteen at this hospital. I saw him doing the mental math, then his eyes shot open and he looked up at me and said, "Whoa!! Thirty-three days?!?!" Whoa indeed!!

Harry is just in the last few days at the point where he can understand and remember things that we tell him. I told him today how numerous your prayers are for him. I reminded him about the CaringBridge website. I told him that there are nine thousand visits to the website, and over four hundred guestbook entries. I have almost sixteen hundred personal emails to share with him, dozens of cards to read to him, a long list of phone messages to tell him about, and gifts for him to enjoy. I've begun reading to him some of the beautiful things that you have written to him, and I wish you could see his face when I do! He is *so* touched and surprised by your outpouring of love.

About a week ago, in one of the guestbook entries, Kimberly wrote, "Never close your eyes to the blessings, the life changing moments, that He will surround you with during these times."

Kimberly, I've printed your advice and hung it on the wall in Harry's room. It's had such an impact on me. Every time I look at it, I think about the blessings and the life-changing moments that God has surrounded us with in the last thirty-three days. For every horrible thing that has happened to Harry, there are hundreds of blessings ... not the least of which is hearing from all of you. Friendships that will last a lifetime have been forged in these life-changing moments. And, we've all shared the witnessing of the miracle of Harry's survival—both a blessing *and* a life-changing moment. Thank you....

Cathy

"I could not go to bed without responding to your beautiful chronicle and message today, Cathy! We have truly witnessed God's blessing in many ways. The most wonderful of those blessings is Harry's miraculous daily recovery! One day he will have to share with us what it is like to stand at the door of both life and death. I envision that one day he will recollect those difficult days when his life hung in the balance. Won't that be something to remember? We wish you wellness, Harry, and our prayers are that you will be home sooner than expected. Cannot wait to see you all again!!! Go 33 1/3!!!!! Wow ... when I saw those numbers again, it reminded me of the scripture in Jeremiah 33:3— 'Call to me and I will answer you and tell you great and unsearchable things you do not know.' (NIV)—that just confirms that the day will come when Harry will remember much!! God Bless You Guys!!!"

~JH

"My brother filled us in on Harry's condition a few days ago and we were both shocked and relieved. Good God, what you all have been through! Miracles do happen every day and God was shining His healing light and strength on Harry during his unspeakable suffering and now during his recovery. The will to live is stronger in some than in others, and it is plain to see Harry is fighting with every fiber to remain here on earth with

his family and friends. With so many people thinking of you every day, you are bound to feel all the love coming your way. You are in our thoughts and prayers and we look forward to hearing about Harry's continued recovery. Our love to you all."
~SC

"I believe Harry's journey has made even the non-believers in miracles True Believers."
~JD

Tuesday, August 25, 2009 2:18 p.m.

The Best Day Yet!

Harry had a really good day today—his best day yet. He had physical therapy this morning, and took many steps down the hall, using a walker, and with only one physical therapist walking along with him. Now, when he moves from bed to a chair, he uses a walker for support, but looks capable of handling the task without assistance. When I think of where he was a week ago, I am in awe of his accomplishments over the last seven days.

The feeding tube nutrients will be tried again tomorrow, and we are really hoping that goes well. Harry is wanting food so badly, as you can imagine! Today, our friend, Batzi, brought him some sugarless gum, in the hopes that he might be able to enjoy it sometime in the future. When she asked the nurse if he could have it now, she said that he could. When he tried the first piece, his eyes glazed over with the enjoyment of the first bit of flavor in his mouth in thirty-four days! He said it tasted like the best meal he has ever had!! Batzi brought him four flavors and he enjoyed every one of them!

Harry was more lucid today than in any of the past days. He has a pain med patch that releases a small amount of medication every hour. Although he can have extra pain relief, he hasn't needed any for almost two days, and I believe this is what is helping to keep his mental status from being so foggy. He had a nice balance today of mental alertness and healthy nap-time. I know I say this every night, but his sense of humor is alive and well. It's so delightful to share many laughs with him throughout the day!

This afternoon, I ran into the nurse (Britanny) that administered Harry's first dialysis treatment here. She stopped in her tracks when she saw me and said, "What are you doing here? Don't tell me that your husband is on this floor already?!" When I told her that he was and that she could go say hello to him, she said she had to see him for herself. She had tears in her eyes when she came into his room. She was astounded at the progress he has made in two weeks. Just fourteen days after arriving here in very serious condition, he is walking, talking, cracking jokes,

and asking for food. She reminded me that on the evening Harry was brought in, there was a question as to whether or not he would make it through the night. She told me that when she met Harrison early the next day, she immediately began praying for Harry, because she thought that his beautiful son needed to have his father with him for many, many more years. Britanny is yet another believer in the miracle of Harry's survival!
Cathy

"There isn't a day that has gone by since we first heard of your ordeal that we don't speak of you or pray for you. My husband wanted me to tell you, Harry, that he donated blood in those early days and discovered that you and he have the same blood type. He hopes you got some of his blood and wants to know if you are now speaking with an Italian accent!"
~CO

"I can barely read because of the tears of joy in my eyes. May God continue to bless you both."
~JW

"We are so thankful God has answered everyone's prayers by putting His healing hand on you and your family. During the early morning quiet time, it has been refreshing to understand how God's love affects all things. Proverbs 18:10 says, 'The name of the Lord is a strong tower, the righteous go to him for safety.' How cool is it that God's promise in the Bible has been lived out every day by your and your families' testimony of faith? We love you guys,"
~MW

"God can, and has, worked miracles and this is one."
~JS

"Following your incredible journal each night before I go to bed has often brought me to tears, but tonight the tears have

a smile behind them. I am thrilled to hear the wonderful news of Harry's progress! Your story about the nurse tonight brought back many beautiful memories of my time with my husband at that hospital. There is truly something very, very special about the staff there. I will never forget our experience there from the brilliant and compassionate doctors to the caring janitor mopping the floors, who smiled and asked how I was doing and reminded me that I was in good hands, at midnight!! It surely made a tough battle just a little bit easier."
~SD

"So I check every day waiting for Cathy to tell us all how you are, Harry. It's funny to think that it wasn't long ago that we were all on a baseball field watching the kids play All-Stars, helping out in that darn snack bar, and just laughing—I can't help but think now how quick time goes by and now, after reading everything you have all been through, how we all need to just really cherish all the little things—yes, I guess even the snack bar!!!"
~LK

"I will be so happy when I read that you are back home where you belong! And, I can't wait for you to read all these postings! You are a truly blessed man ... all your loving ways have been redirected back to you ... awesome!!"
~JJ

Wednesday, August 26, 2009 11:50 p.m.

A Huge Step!

Harry has had an NG (nasogastric) tube in place for almost five weeks. The tube goes through the nose, down the throat, and into the stomach, to remove stomach acid and secretions while a patient isn't consuming food. (Sorry to be so graphic—hope you haven't just finished dinner!) This morning, Harry's NG tube was removed (a huge step!), because his intestines are *finally* beginning to function. He was able to drink clear liquids today—diluted cranberry juice, vegetable broth and chicken broth. He said it tasted as delicious as Thanksgiving dinner! And he was just as stuffed....

Getting away from IV nutrition is such a good thing. IV nutrition is mostly metabolized in the liver—not a good thing when the liver is already struggling. IV nutrition also has a lot of sugar, so balancing the blood sugar with insulin injections is something that needs to be addressed every four hours. And, the IV nutrition is a bit pricey—*$2,000 per day*!! Natural mouth to stomach nutrition will jump-start everything that needs a boost right now—the liver, kidneys, intestines, brain and muscles. This first step towards normal food consumption really is a big one.

Surgery to begin closing the abdomen is scheduled for Friday afternoon. It probably can't be closed all the way just yet, but the doctor will make that decision during the surgery. Another step closer to going home!

Harry walked down the hall today—such a major accomplishment for someone who could barely stand with assistance just nine days ago. He is able to adjust his position in bed, lies on his side, and sits up as if his abs were actually intact!

Yesterday, when someone asked us what happened, I looked at Harry and asked if he was ready to hear the story. He said he was, and I agreed with him. I didn't give him the thirty second version. I told him many more details than he had already heard. The *entire* story is still weeks away, but for now, he undoubtedly understands how seriously ill he has been. Some of the non-medical details I included were about how the "troops have rallied around him," about the prayers that have brought him back from the brink of death. I told him about the many friends who have made our lives so much easier with their help, and about the support of his loving family.

Harry's brother, Bill, and his beautiful wife, Kathi, flew in today from Colorado. I'll never forget the look on Kathi's face when she saw him—such joy at the transformation of the Harry from weeks ago! And, when Bill bent down to kiss Harry on the cheek, Harry raised both his arms (not easy to do with IVs and monitors everywhere!) to bring Bill back for a big, big hug. He said, "Thank you, Billy. I know you helped save my life."
Cathy

"Although we have only met briefly on a few occasions, because you have both been so close to my brother, Dave, for all these years, we feel friendship and caring for your welfare and happiness. Reading your last journal entry filled my heart with such overwhelming joy! Harry is so lucky to have you, his family and so many friends all praying for his recovery—and it seems to be working! Please tell him that even distant acquaintances, like us, are thinking of him and hoping his 'larger than life' presence continues to surface from the depths of his suffering. I look forward to your next journal entry!"
~SC

"I think perhaps this might be a good time to consider putting in that pool, so you can go home, sit by the pool, have that margarita, and invite us all over to celebrate your homecoming!"
~MK

"It is with ongoing amazement that I have read of Harry's progress and, even more, your incredible strength through all this. Plus, you are approaching the point where the networks will want you as their medical correspondent. :-)"
~BP

"We are SO happy to hear of the amazing progress of the last few days. We have been following Harry's incredible story each day, through your inspiring updates. My husband has shared many stories with me about Harry, his contagious smile, his quick wit, and the love for his son that radiates in every ounce of him. Each night I read your journal entry and I am compelled to sign this guestbook, but when I saw the photo from a few nights ago of Harrison and Harry, it brought tears to my eyes. I am fast forwarding four years to Harrison walking across the stage at his high school graduation, and predicting the look of pride on Harry's face! Please know that the three of you are in our thoughts constantly, and if there is anything we can do, we would love to do it. We wish you many more 'best days yet!'
With much love,"
~LA

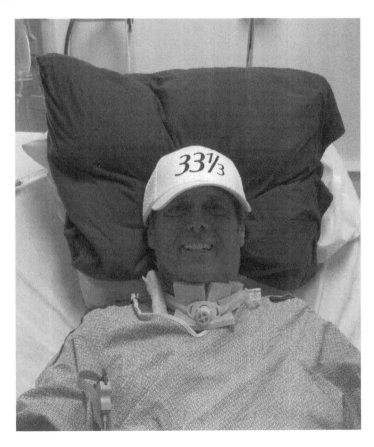

Thursday, August 27, 2009 Midnight and Beyond

Five Weeks Ago Today ...

SO much has happened in these five weeks! We are nearing the end of the journey, though, because Harry is making great progress every day. Today was another good day—no dialysis, but lots of rest, some exercise, a bit of nutrition, and a few laughs—sounds like a good day, does it not?

Harry walked around the 6th floor—twice today. He didn't need assistance, but used the walker for "just in case." He enjoyed several clear liquids that I brought for him—fresh squeezed OJ, pure apple juice, and organic chicken broth. He took some nutritional supplements that brother Bill brought for him, and seemed to get better by the minute.

Do you remember Dr. 33 1/3%? Harry is now officially the only patient in hospital history to survive "abdominal compartment syndrome." Our friends George and Lene Marie sent caps to Harry, Harrison, and me with "33 1/3" on them! We will forever wear them proudly! Thank you, George and Lene! XOXO

I didn't want to leave Harry tonight. For the last hour and a half that we were together, we cuddled on the bed, talked, laughed, and watched some baseball and football on TV. Over the last couple of days, Harry has learned so much more about what happened to him. (Just today, we told him about how he was in danger of losing his foot—and you should have seen his face when he heard that story!) He is amazed, but humbled by how serious his situation was for so many days. He said tonight that nothing else matters, but being alive and enjoying our family life together. My thoughts exactly!
Cathy

"Your story only touches a small part in life at what God can do when people make the right choices. In marriage, in friendship, in love. Thank you for sharing every day. Thank you for the picture. Harry, I am happy for you and I miss you. I cried again tonight because I have not seen you since the

football meeting. I wanted to stay away and allow you to heal. With great love and thankfulness,"
~DR

"Cathy, I just love your updates. You are so good at relaying details and keeping us abreast of Harry's progression. No matter how tired I am, I have to click on this website to see how everyone is doing. Wow, Harry ... you are amazing. What a strong man you are and what a fantastic family you all have. Our prayers are for your continued progress and peace for your wonderful family. We sure miss seeing you all out and about and we know it won't be long before we see your smiling faces.
Take care and God Bless,"
~GM

"Oh, Dear Harry, I am so thrilled to hear of your progress. It brought tears to my eyes. Tomorrow I will call Tim and Dick and give a full report. We seldom realize how much of an impact we have on other people's lives. Your kindheartedness and genuine friendship have always been an inspiration to me. I look forward to your complete recovery! God bless you and your wonderful family!"
~BJM

"Harry, After such an ordeal that you've been through, you still look as handsome as you were in high school forty-two years ago. As for Harrison ... I have to say he is a bit more handsome than you were ... of course ... with Cathy's genes. Cathy, though I've never had the pleasure of meeting you yet, you are the one who has brought both Harry's and your friends close into your family. We have all shared your despair and your joy all along the journey. Reading your journal has become part of my daily life now ... what am I going to do when Harry goes home and is up running around ??"
~SK

"Harry looks better after all this than most of us do daily with no surgery. :-}"
~JC

"Oh my, it is so good to see a picture of Harry smiling! For a while there, it was something we thought we would never see again. Your entry today and hearing that Harry is doing so well gave me the chills! That you could walk down the hall without help, that you cuddled with your beautiful wife, and that you talked for hours brought tears to my eyes. We are so thankful for your recovery and we want you to know that we love you guys! It's been too long since we have seen you three and we look forward to the next time. Rest lots, smile lots and like you said, Harry, 'your family love is the best recipe for happiness!!'"
~KM

Friday, August 28, 2009 Well After Midnight

All Closed!

Harry had his abdominal surgery this afternoon, and now he is completely closed! His surgeon was so pleased that he was able to close him all the way in one surgery instead of two—once again something unexpected. He developed some bleeding and a fever while in recovery, and went back in to surgery at 8:30 tonight to deal with the bleeding. Luckily, it was all subcutaneous, not internal bleeding. Tonight his signs are stable. He will go back to CCU around midnight, and just for the night. Harry calls it "the sleep deprivation chamber," but I'm sure it won't be a problem for him tonight, as he is sleepy with sedation. Pain will be an issue for a couple of days, as you can imagine. But now the organs can be expected to function more efficiently, so we are well on our way to going home! A little more healing and recovery....

His kidney function numbers were so good this morning that he didn't need dialysis—a day that he would normally have needed it. Before the surgery, Harry was feeling really good. He was hungry, though, and couldn't have anything before surgery, but is looking forward to some juice and broth on Sunday and soft food soon after that.

Harrison finished his two-a-day football practices today. Two busy weeks! The team moms topped off the team's accomplishments by hosting a barbecue for all of the families tonight at the conclusion of the final practice at 7:30 p.m.. It was a festive, energetic celebration of all of the hard work that the coaches and players have put in over the last two weeks.

Happy Weekend,

Cathy

Saturday, August 29, 2009 5:57 p.m.

Harry is Amazing!

Harry had a rough night last night. After he came out of surgery at 4:30 p.m., he was alert and talking and for a while all was well. His blood pressure got lower and lower, and he spiked a high fever. Remember that the last time his blood pressure dropped dramatically, it caused his kidneys to shut down. And, low blood pressure can be a sign of bleeding ... something with which we are painfully familiar. It was a challenging four hours, and finally the decision was made to go back to the OR to see where the suspected bleeding was. It turned out to be only at the incision—bleeding just under the skin. An old hematoma that was removed in the earlier surgery is suspected to be the source of bacteremia, that caused the high fever. By 10:30 last night, doctors were still "concerned." He finally made it to his room in CCU at midnight.

Last night, at the football barbecue, Coach Welch talked about, among other things, his appreciation for the volunteer work and support of the families, and the philosophy and goals of the coaching staff and the football program. He talked about the team doctor, Dr. Newton (a graduate of the school and an anesthesiologist), but Tom was unable to be there. He also talked very graciously about Harry, thanked everyone for their continued prayers, and encouraged them to sign a beautiful poster made by the team moms. Little did anyone know at the time ... right when Coach Welch was speaking about them—Harry was in his second surgery, and his attending anesthesiologist was ... Tom Newton!

When the phone rang at 6:45 this morning, I felt the all too familiar stomach drop. It was *Harry*, letting me know that he was doing better. I was already up, getting ready to take Harrison to football practice, so once my heart slowed down, I was able to be relieved at his news. Harry really is doing better today. His temp is 98.8, he looks good, is talking, and eating ice chips again. He is in a great deal of pain, which is expected, so pain meds are greatly appreciated and in plentiful supply today.

Harry's kidney function is so good today, that he does not

need dialysis—for the third day in a row. He may be past the
need for it at all. His liver functions also continue to improve.
He has been breathing very well on his own—even through
both surgeries, and he may have the tracheotomy tube taken out
on Monday. Tonight, he will be moved back to sub-ICU (better
sleep, yay!), and I will stay with him much later than usual,
because Harrison is going to the Angels game with friends. He
can go back to clear liquids tomorrow, and is anxious to progress
from there. If all goes well this weekend, and early in the week—
he might be coming home by the end of the week!!
 Now that we are back in CCU, we are seeing all of the
personnel that worked on Harry while he was there for two
weeks. Most of them cannot believe the rapid progress that he
has made, and all are so happy to see his improvement. They all
say the same thing—"Harry is amazing!"
Cathy

On Friday afternoon, when Harry went into surgery, I had fully
expected to see him in recovery before I left for the football banquet. I
debated whether or not to even go to the banquet. All of the doctors and
nurses encouraged me to do so, telling me how good it would be for me
to get out and to be surrounded by friends who had been so supportive
during this ordeal. I knew as well that it would be very important for me
to be there for Harrison; and I wanted to be there for him. Harry agreed
with me and encouraged me to go and to enjoy myself.

Unfortunately, Harry was not yet out of surgery when it was time for
me to leave for the banquet. The nurses kept telling me to just go and that
they would text or call if they needed anything. They kept reassuring me
that he was in good hands.

I had turned off my phone when I got into the car for the drive to the
school. I put on piano music and tried to relax and focus on enjoying
myself for the next few hours. When I got to the parking lot and turned
my phone back on, there were three phone messages and nine text
messages … all from the hospital! This wasn't the first time that my
stomach sank and my heart rate skyrocketed. I called the hospital and
was told by the nurse that Harry had developed some bleeding and a
fever when he got into recovery. The vascular surgeon had been called

back to the hospital (as he had just left) and they were planning to take Harry back into surgery to address the bleeding.

Dr. Newton, the anesthesiologist and football team doctor, was working that afternoon and was in recovery checking on some of his patients. His back was turned to Harry at the time, but he saw Harry's arterial blood spurt past him across the room. When he turned and saw who it was that was bleeding, he just couldn't believe it. He rushed over to him and laid across his abdomen to staunch the flow of blood. He immediately and urgently asked for the nurses to call the surgeon back to the hospital. Harry was perhaps the calmest of everybody in the room. After everything he had been through, what was a little arterial spurt? As I mentioned in the update, the bleeding was just surface bleeding from the incision site and was easily fixed. The staff also dealt effectively with his fever. By the time he got to a room, he was understandably exhausted from the afternoon and evening's activity.

That evening, I found myself once again in the pretend mode. I'd like to think that on the surface I looked calm and hopeful. I certainly wanted Harrison to see me that way and I wanted our friends to take a signal from me that everything was going to be okay. I definitely didn't feel that way on the inside. I was worried and wanting to be back in the hospital, even if it was just to sit in the waiting room and see Harry for five minutes with my own eyes after he got into his room. I didn't go back to the hospital that night. I took Harrison home from the banquet, hid my concern and apprehension, and just enjoyed my time with him. After a late night update from Harry's nurse, I was comforted by the fact that he was doing okay and that we would see him first thing the next morning. I fell asleep that night feeling very peaceful that he truly was on his way.

Sunday, August 30, 2009 11:47 p.m.

Better and Better ...

Last night, when I left the hospital at 10:45, it was hard for me to imagine that Harry would be well enough to go home by the end of this week. Yesterday was difficult for Harry because of the pain in his abdomen. Even with medication, the pain never dropped below a five on a pain scale of zero to ten.

But, today, Harry was doing much better. His pain was more manageable, he walked three times, and started back on clear liquids. And ... *the tracheotomy tube was removed this afternoon!!* His kidney function numbers and liver numbers are the best today that they have been since his admission to this hospital nineteen days ago. If the numbers improve again tomorrow, he will most likely have the dialysis ports in his neck removed tomorrow or Tuesday. Most of the doctors feel that his need for dialysis is now a thing of the past!

The goal for the next few days will be to focus on nutrition and exercise. A little different from a few weeks ago, huh? He still has a long way to go with both, but knowing Harry, he will surprise us all with his daily progress. And, going home by the end of the week?... *maybe so?...*

The journey is almost at its end. Thank you for traveling with me through both the happy and difficult days. You truly have boosted my strength with your love, and your many prayers helped saved Harry's life. Of that, I have absolutely no doubt.

Tonight, as I write this, I am sitting next to Harry's bed, watching the sunset with him from his ocean view room! It gives me great pleasure to say that tonight's closing comes from the two of us. We wish you a good week, and we thank you ... for everything!

Harry and Cathy

"Oh my goodness!!! Joy! Joy! Joy! We read the updates regularly!!! What a fabulous idea this website is! I apologize we haven't signed in before. Cathy, you know we love you all and think of you every day. Can't tell you in words how happy

we are to hear our fabulous 'Coach' of baseball and life is walking around. Watch out world ... you haven't seen nothing yet!"
~TZ

"Your healing is inspiring, Harry, and YOU LOOK MAAAUUVELOUS!!! Cathy, thank you for all the daily updates ... they help us in knowing the specifics to pray for each of you."
~JH

"I remember reading somewhere that it is so easy for us to see the face of God in nature, and yet so difficult for us to see God's face in our fellow man. I look at the photo of you in that white hat and I see the face of God shining out at us through your wonderful smile. You are the best!"
~MK

"Just a few days ago was the first time I heard about what happened to Dr. White. I have to admit that I have spent the last two hours sobbing and reading about the terrible nightmare your family has had to endure over these past weeks. But I have to clarify the first several entries left me sobbing with sadness and fear about Harry's prognosis, but while reading the last couple of weeks' entries, I found myself crying out of happiness and excitement about how well our dear "Dr. White" has been doing. After every beautifully scripted entry from Cathy, I found myself (as un-religious as I am) saying, 'Thank God.' This world is so much better with Harry White in it and I am so glad that God realizes that we need him here for years and years to come to continue to put smiles on our faces (and straight toothed smiles, at that!)."
~JVT

"You know how it feels when the rain begins to gently fall after a long absence of it? That's what it feels like right now knowing that you are going to live, Harry. Your life is never going to be the same again—it's going to be much better now!

One day, when you return home and the rain begins to fall, walk outside and lift your face toward it because it is living water and you are a living miracle! You are 33 1/3. Your life is now another man's hope of living! Love and blessings go out tonight, may you sleep peacefully even in the place of 'no rest!'"
~JH

"I count reading your daily updates a highlight of my mornings. Your honest and loving details of Harry's 'adventure' bring me so often to tears, and then smiles, and then deep gratitude for God's great goodness and His powerful presence in your lives. What a testimony you both are to Love, in all of its glorious forms. Love and be loved,"
~JF

Monday, August 31, 2009 Midnight

40 Days and 40 Nights

It's official! HARRY WILL NO LONGER NEED DIALYSIS!!!! It was just three weeks ago that he was admitted to this hospital, and I can still remember the feeling I had when our intensivist told us that he was afraid that Harry would need dialysis for the rest of his life. Today, his dialysis catheter was removed and his kidneys are working *and* improving. Such a huge step!!

I was told that the tracheotomy site is expected to heal quickly, but I became a believer today when the dressing over the site was changed, and I saw that in less than twenty-four hours—it is almost closed! There are no sutures, the one-inch incision closes on its own. I know—you are shaking your head at that one! I am, too.

Harry is off IV pain meds, taking them only by pill form now. His only two IVs are an antibiotic (which can be switched to pill form), and his expensive nutrients. When the nutrient bag finishes tonight, there will be no more to replace it. He passed his swallow evaluation for soft foods today, and has had juice, rice, sourdough bread, and a bite of salmon tonight. By tomorrow, he may be able to kiss the IV pole goodbye!

Exercise is key in Harry's recovery, and today he walked without a walker. He took five different excursions—all around the nurses' station. When I realize that it was less than seventy-two hours since his abdominal surgery, I am amazed at and proud of the progress he has made. He is so strong and determined to return to the life he loves!

Today, when I was telling two dear friends about Harry's struggles of the past forty days and forty nights, we all shared the same thought—that Harry's survival is a miracle. Harry's friend, Dennis, from high school, has dubbed him "The Miracle Man." I still wonder at the possibility that Harry will be able to leave the hospital by the end of the week, but if anyone can, it will be *The Miracle Man*!
Cathy

"Dear Harry, You indeed are the "miracle man!" All of your family, your friends and your clients have now truly witnessed the POWER of prayer!! We thank Cathy for keeping us updated on your progress and when you are well enough to read what she has shared, her anguish, her joys, YOU owe her one fabulous vacation! :-)"
~BJM

"Forty days and forty nights ... a coincidence? I think not. Best wishes on your continued healing process, H."
~DB

"I have been following Harry's story, and as a nurse I really know how seriously ill he has been and what a miracle it is that he has made the progress that he has made so far. I know that your love and your courage, Cathy, have made all the difference. And I am sure that your strong bond has been made stronger by this joint battle. I will send my love and healing energy toward you both, each and every day until Harry is well. I hope that Jim and I can take you both out for a lovely dinner, once Harry is all back together again. He is really amazing and I think 33 1/3 underestimates it by a significant bit ... it should be more like 1 in a million. Love to you and your family. Thanks for turning me on to CaringBridge, I will recommend it to my patient families. It is a great site."
~VH

"This has indeed been quite an unexpected journey. We have followed and read each post every night. Thanks for keeping us so well informed. Harry, through all you've been through, you still look great!! The progress you've made this last week has been incredible. We are thrilled and thankful that you are heading towards a successful and full recovery. The positive impact you have both made on so many people's lives is evident by the outpouring of love and support you've received from this site alone. Over 11,600 visits!! You are in our daily thoughts and prayers. Keep up the good work ... looking forward to hearing about your homecoming."
~MM

"It is great to hear of Harry's progress and I am sure he will progress even more dramatically this upcoming week. Our hope and prayers are lifted up for him going home by the week's end. Our toast for you tonight is that 'May you enjoy thousands and thousands of sunsets together!'"
~DW

"You remind me of a quote from a little book you once gave me, Dr. White. 'Never give up on anybody. Miracles happen every day.' Remember, the greatest distance you have yet to cover still lies within you but with your host of 'raving fans' you can't go wrong...."
~JB

"Angels danced the day you were born, and have made sure all of your family and friends could enjoy you a while longer. Harry, may your road to recovery continue at a rapid pace, may each and every person your journey has touched remember to take a few moments each day to pray for others less fortunate and thank God for being alive."
~DT

It was during this week, when Harry was in this beautiful room with a view of the ocean, that he began talking about ... *Reykjavik*. I was convinced that these were drug-induced ramblings. Yet, day after day, he would talk in detail about the ports and marinas and hills and roads of Reykjavik. I would patiently remind him that the water he saw was the Pacific Ocean, not the waters of Iceland. He persisted insistently about all of these details involving Reykjavik.

Harry has never been to Iceland, but I found it intriguing that he seemed so sure of himself, regarding the geography of the coastline. It would be several weeks before his fine motor skill had returned enough for him to write or draw legibly. But a few weeks after he got home, I brought up the subject of Reykjavik. He, of course, remembered talking about it while in the hospital. I asked if he would draw a map of what he remembered about the coastline, marina, roads, etc. He enthusiastically agreed to do so. His drawing was quite detailed and he never hesitated or questioned himself as he drew. When he finished, we went to the computer and brought up Reykjavik on our computer's map. Harry's drawing was exactly the coastline … of Reykjavik!

Tuesday, September 1, 2009 2:48 p.m.

The First Time in Forty-one Days ...

For the first time in forty-one days, Harry is not connected to an IV pole! What freedom! All medication is now taken orally. Full function of his kidneys and liver should return within the next two weeks. He ate a variety of healthy foods (scrambled eggs, watermelon, banana smoothie, turkey, cheese) today, but very, very small portions of each. It's been so long since he had a normal meal, that he gets full on just a bite or a few sips.

Also, for the first time in forty-one days, Harry shaved himself. It exhausted him, but he did it. He walked five times today—the last four times, without his IV pole, and with no assistance. For the first time in forty-one days—*Harry enjoyed fresh air*! On one of his walks, the therapist took him to a balcony door, and he took in the warm, moist, beach air. You should have seen the look on his face. Such a simple thing that we all take for granted! He loved it.

Harry developed an intestinal infection, so we had to don protection while in his room today. Tonight's photo is of our friend Dougall and Harrison. Dougall never fails to make Harry laugh, as he did today in his 'sanitation garb.' Over the last three days, we tried not to say anything that

would make Harry laugh, because it hurt so much for him to do so. Like everything else, laughing is getting easier. Harry is making remarkable progress.

Although Harry normally loves to read, he hasn't done any of it yet, because it sounds too tiring to him. So, instead, I have been reading to him, and he enjoys it. I've read some cards and some emails and guestbook entries. Today, I read him my journal entries from July 23rd to August 1st. It was tough to get through some of it, especially the entries on July 31st. He is shocked at what happened to him, and amazed that he is still here. And, he can't wait for the next ten pages of journal entries tomorrow. For the first time in forty-one days, Harry truly understands why his journey of survival has been so long and so difficult.

Harry will have a CT scan on Thursday to check his abdomen. If all is well with that, he most likely will be released from the hospital on *Friday*!! I know he wants so very badly to go to Harrison's game at 11:00 a.m. on Saturday, but it's hard for me to envision that right now. He has come so far in his recovery, but he still has a long way to go. He gets worn out just sitting in a chair having a couple of bites of food. I can't imagine him getting dressed, riding twenty minutes to school, watching the game for two hours, then heading home—just too much. I know, I know—he's driven, he's strong, and you can't keep a good man down! We shall see....
The Whites

"I heard a wonderful quote this evening and I have to share it with you. 'We do not need more things in which to be thankful ... but instead to be thankful for more things!' I know your list of things in which to be thankful for grows by the day. You must be feeling like God's favorite right now, and guess what ... you are! Many, many blessings as you continue to come through this remarkably well!"
~JH

"I was shocked to hear the details of Harry's plight recently and have spent the past hour and a half reading all of your

*entries in this journal. I am struck by how very ill your strong
Harry has been. I could never imagine this would happen to
a guy such as he! Never in a million years! It does not at all
surprise me that so many people have shown their love and
support for this wonderful man, as he has, for so many years,
shown his love and support for us through his sweet birthday
calls and his sincere words of kindness ... and oh yes, his
infectious smile!!!"*
~KR

*"Dear Harry, Each new journal report is so encouraging that
all I can say is PRAISE THE LORD! My friend, you are one
tough hombre, especially when you don't shave! Now get your
butt home Friday and be at Harrison's game on Saturday!
Seriously, I am praying that you will be there! Give Cathy a
hug and a big kiss for me ... she has been your greatest asset!
Hope to see you soon....Your Sedan buddy ... "*
~BJM

*"Dear Cathy & Harry, The kids and I have just got back from
NY. I had no access to any computer there—hard to believe,
but true. I had told my family all about you and how precious
life really is. Before that I looked forward to your daily report
on Harry's unbelievable path to recovery. It was the last thing
I did before going to bed. When Paul visited he told me that
Harry was doing really well. I couldn't believe it. It took
my breath away. I sit here this morning, reading each day I
missed. I couldn't be more happy and astonished for you and
all your families. Harry you are TRULY the Miracle Man.
Can't wait for the day I see you at a community event to see
that smile in person and exchange a great big Hug. God Bless
ya, Harry."*
~CW

Back from Code Blue

Wednesday, September 2, 2009

Thumbs Up to That!

Harry has eleven specialists that have attended to him while in the hospital. When his internist saw Harry today, he told him that his recovery is nothing short of miraculous, and that cases like Harry's are why he went into medicine. Just three weeks ago, Harry was in the midst of total organ failure ... and, now ... he is almost ready to go home. This afternoon, when Harry asked me what I was planning to write about in tonight's update, I told him "*Batzi.*" He smiled, gave me the thumbs up, closed his eyes and said, "Perfect!!"

I can't begin to imagine what I would have done these past six weeks without Batzi. Batzi has done so much for us—she has cooked meals (for us *and* for friends of ours), driven Harrison to and from football practice, taken him to order his school uniform, fed and walked our dogs, and done grocery shopping for us. When Harry's brother, Bill, spent his birthday with us at the hospital (August 4th), Batzi brought him a delicious birthday cake, and presented him with a beautifully wrapped, thoughtful gift. When Helen celebrated her 86th birthday, there was a lovely, sentimental gift from Batzi. She bought me the sweetest gift of comfort, and presented Harry with his sugarless gum!! He'll never forget how wonderful that tasted!

Batzi has a great sense of humor. Even after some of our more difficult days, Batzi could make me laugh, and it was refreshingly therapeutic. One night, while visiting Harry, she asked him if it was okay to come see him the next day, and he said, "As long as you're funny!" Batzi has spent *countless hours* with me at the hospital. The first night, when Harry was in surgery until 1:30 a.m., Batzi was there with me. The morning after Harry's awful CPR incident, Batzi came over to be with me, because she didn't want Harrison and me to be alone. She wouldn't let me drive by myself for several days after that. Not a day goes by without help from her.

It isn't just that Batzi does these things for us—it's also the way she does them. She seems to know what I need almost before I do. She loves our son as if he were one of her own. She's treated my friends and family as if they are friends of hers. She offers her help with so much love, so much caring. The three of us love her very, very much!

I honestly don't know how people survive tragedies without friends like Batzi, and without family. I can only imagine the physical and emotional exhaustion of dealing with each day alone, and I find that incredibly sad. I thank God every day for Batzi, for our many wonderful friends, and for Harry's family and mine.

Cathy and the Boys

"Although this is in tribute to my brother-in-law, Harry, whose life and health I cherish, I can't resist adding a word or two about Batzi. While Cathy and Bill tended to the business of seeing that Harry got the best possible care available, I sat in the waiting room with my dear parents-in-law, awesome family members, other wonderful visitors, and of course, Batzi. There was an instant connection! This is everyone's dream 'person,' if you know what I mean. Her presence is such a comfort. She knows just what to say, and when. And she's sincere. She's been around life's block once or twice, and because of that, she's right there with you. I feel like I've known her a good long while, and I guess I have Harry and Cathy to thank for that. (Harry, you didn't have to go to this extent!!) Batzi, we'll see you again and again...."
~KW

"My, my ... what wonderful news continues to come through your journal! We are elated for the progress, though we know baby steps are in order. But God has already done MIRACULOUS things here, and we will continue to believe that he is not done yet! So, I won't rule out anything about Harrison's ball game on Saturday ... who thought you'd be this far along five days ago?! As for Batzi, wouldn't this be a perfect world if everyone had just one friend like her?"
~LH

"Batzi is truly an angel! Some of that love that helps miracles happen!!"
~NE

"Batzi, Thank you so much for making this very difficult journey easier for our dear friends the Whites. We know how hard it is seeing someone you love SO much be so sick. It is friends like you who get us through the bad news and hard nights. You keep the faith with us even when others have lost it. A friendship like you and the Whites have is a huge and often rare blessing! From ALL of the White fans out here, we THANK YOU!!!"
~SB

"I will never forget Batzi. Her story, her generosity, her kindness were unforgettable."
~JH

"Thank you Batzi for making life easier for Cathy and the whole family. My next door neighbor's house is for sale? LOL"
~HF

"A word for Batzi ~ Thank you for being there for the beautiful, amazing White Family. Thank you for knowing what to do, for your time, energy and support ... for being there on behalf of all of us who love Harry, Cathy and Harrison. By Cathy's words we know you are a rare and wonderful gift. Thank you."
~CP

Thursday, September 3, 2009

Closer and Closer to Home ...

Thank you to all of you who donated blood in Harry's honor today for the Red Cross drive!!!

Thank you, Dr. Zachary, for all you did to make the Red Cross Blood Drive in Harry's honor such a success yesterday!

Harry's infection has been managed and he is now officially out of quarantine. His CT scan from this morning showed a small amount of fluid accumulation in the lower right portion of his abdomen, but it isn't expected to be problematic. Other than that, everything else looks good. The kidney and liver numbers continue to improve, as has Harry's appetite and mobility. (He tackled twelve stairs today!) It is with the greatest pleasure that I can share the good news:

HARRY IS COMING HOME TOMORROW!!!

In following doctor's recommendations, visitors are not allowed for a while after Harry arrives home. First and most importantly, Harry needs to sleep. Also, he is under the risk of infection, as his twenty inch, fifty-eight metal-staple incision is open to the air and is still seeping a bit. Harrison and I will be busy helping Harry with all of the many tasks that have been handled in the past forty-four days by the hospital's wonderful medical personnel, and we need time to adjust to our new family schedule. Thank you for your patience and understanding. I'll let you know when visiting is an option.

This afternoon, I read to Harry the eight-page letter that Harrison wrote to him on July 23rd. We both shed quite a few tears during the reading. Afterwards, we talked about how incredibly blessed we are and how we cannot *wait* to be together as a family again. Soon....

So looking forward to tomorrow!

Harry, Cathy and Harrison

"WOW! I just found out about your trip to hell and back. I want you to know that over the years, I have thought about you from time to time. Although I'm sure you didn't realize this, but you have had a tremendous impact upon my life. Not only for what you did to help me orthodontically, when no other ortho could or would, but also because from the first day I met you, I sensed something very special and extraordinary about you as a human being. Harry: you are a wonderful father, husband, doctor and human being who has made this world a better place for SO many people. You make me want to be a better man. And for that, I love you. Hurry up and get better so you and your wife can double date with me and my gal at a really great concert...."
~AB

"Harry, you stay home and rest. I will be at the game yelling for all the boys and embarrassing most. God Bless and please leave the yelling, louder than most, to me. I will scream, 'Harrison Good Job Dude.'"
~DR

"Hi Harry, You look pretty damn good now that the tube is out of your nose and the other one is out of your neck! It won't be long before your pecs are jumping, just like in the old days when you used to try to show up the skinny guys. I heard from our old friend Raul today ... all the way from Panama. I haven't heard a peep from him for forty years. And so many of the other "amici" from Italy have been writing, sending their best wishes to you. Another silver lining to the black cloud of your ordeal! Your amazing journey to the brink of extinction and back has beckoned lots of old friends to reconnect, and remember their beloved old pal Harry. Ain't life grand?"
~KW

"Hold on to this time—don't forget the good and the miracles—this time will be a testimony to others."
~AT

"From tragedy to triumph ... I have read each and every word of Harry's journey with such a range of emotion ... from shock, disbelief, sadness and anguish to joy, thankfulness, and elation! I have cried, worried, laughed and cheered ... sometimes all in the same day! This has been a story of love and the power of faith, and everyone who has read your words has marveled at your strength and eloquence. I love happy endings, and this has been one of the best ones I have heard in a long, long time! Life and love are so very precious, and the greatest gift you can give your family. Harry, take your time and recover fully. No matter when it is, the first game you attend will certainly be Harrison's most memorable one of the season! Thinking and praying for you!
With love,"
~LF

"Dear White Family, This has been some story! Non-fiction with ups and downs, tears and laughter, high suspense and sighs of relief, extensive vocabulary and medical terminology, highly articulate daily first-person accounts of events, an incredible cast of characters that we've come to know and love, a courageous, inspiring hero along with a beautiful, astonishing heroine, plus the handsome, athletic son. There were so many dragons to slay and that took the help of countless professionals, family and friends. The main themes included a love story, a hero's journey, being touched by the Divine, prayers and angels, and the mystery: How could this happen to such a nice guy? The best part of all is the 'happy ending,' which we all know is truly just a beginning."
~HN

Friday, September 4, 2009

The Homecoming

I can't begin to tell you how nice it is to have Harry home! We arrived home around 3:00 this afternoon, and the first thing Harry wanted to do was take a shower, a worthy desire for someone who has not had a shower in the last forty-four days! Thanks to some supplies given to us by our wonderful nurses, I was able to waterproof Harry's tracheostomy incision and the abdominal drain. That delightful shower was followed by a light snack and a heavy power nap. Ahhhhhhh … *It is so great to be home!*

It was bittersweet leaving the hospital today. As excited as we were to be heading home, there has been such an emotional attachment to Harry's nurses and doctors, that it was difficult to say goodbye and to adequately express our gratitude to them. How do you thank someone for saving your life, for helping you thrive in your return to health?

Harry and I are having a little at-home date tonight. We are cuddled on the couch, watching the Angels game, but glued to the phone. Harrison is at his high school's varsity football game tonight, but cannot call us, because the JV players are on the sidelines during the game. But, Harry's brother Rolly is in the stands, and giving us frequent updates.

One of the many lessons that the last six weeks have taught us is that *the outcome of this game tonight is really not important*. But the life lessons from this football experience are what have value. The lessons of commitment, hard work, being a team player, and perseverance are what we want our children to learn from sports and school. How blessed are we when mentors guide our children and provide them with experiences and valuable lessons that they will remember for the rest of their lives? We are feeling especially grateful tonight for all of our many, many blessings—faith, family, friends, and yes—football!

Speaking of football—hmmmmm—I don't know yet about the game tomorrow. The trip home today completely exhausted Harry, so we will have to evaluate tomorrow morning. But you can be sure, I will keep you posted!

> **Have I told you lately how happy I am to have Harry home?!? :-))**
> Cathy

Early in Harry's hospitalization, a friend sent me the email below. I didn't realize how profound her words were until the days and weeks after I brought Harry home.

"Cathy, I am so sorry. This all just doesn't make sense, does it? I can tell you that you will get through this, as terrible as it seems right now. I know because I have been in a similar situation when my husband finished his last day of radiation therapy. Some days will be tougher than others, but I promise you, it will get better. I would like to share something with you....

Through everything with my husband, everyone would ask how I was doing and they kept telling me that I needed to take care of myself. I listened but I thought Rick was the one who needed the concern now, not me. As we got through some of the tougher times and things were somewhat easier, I realized, that as a woman that loved her husband, as the caregiver and also having a job, I was somewhat on auto pilot, so I did start doing little things that made me feel better. I am strong and I think I was fine, but I needed to stay that way. I mention this because, for me, the hardest time was when my husband came home!

I definitely wanted him home and knew that recovery would be quicker at home, but I hadn't thought about it completely. I now had him 24/7! When he was in the hospital, I was able to get away for a little bit to get some sleep and regroup, and I knew he was being taken care of. When he came home I listened for any unusual breathing, jumped out of bed when I heard him get up in the middle of the night, and it went on and on! I don't think I had more than one consecutive hour of sleep for at least two weeks. I am not complaining, just sharing my experience and letting you know ... everyone was right—please also take care of yourself through this. Don't

feel guilty about doing little things that make you feel good. You need to stay strong and healthy for him you and Harrison. You will be VERY busy when Harry comes home."
~T

I took the thoughts in this email to heart early on and did take advantage of every opportunity I had to get rest ... ha! ... and enjoy tidbits of time here and there with Harrison, other family members and friends. A few days after I brought Harry home, I remembered this email and actually laughed out loud at how profound Terry's predictions were.

I was elated to be picking Harry up from the hospital. Everything was ready for him at home and I had pillows and a blanket for him in the car. I was giddy with excitement. This, to me, was affirmation that he was going to survive and return to health.

The drive home was difficult for Harry. Every imperfection in the road and driving over a Botts dot made him groan in discomfort. By the time I pulled into the garage, his coloring was a bit gray and he had broken out in a sweat. We waited several minutes before our attempt to go inside. I had the guest room downstairs set up for him, but he wanted to go upstairs to the master bedroom. It must have taken us ten minutes to climb the eighteen steps to the second floor. The first thing he wanted to do was to take a shower and I can't blame him. It had been forty-five days since he had done so. I laid him down on the couch in our bedroom and covered his stapled twenty-inch incision with protective plastic wrap. I then got into the shower with him, had him sit on the bench while I washed his hair and bathed him with the hand-held shower. He groaned again, but this time, it was because it felt so good to have a shower. After drying him off, I walked him over to the sink so he could brush his teeth. As I stood looking at his back, I realized I could have taught an anatomy class, "Skeletal Structure 101," by pointing out all of the bones in his back. He looked like a war refugee. I could see every rib and vertebra. His shoulder blades looked like paddles and his shoulders looked like two tennis balls covered in skin.

Harry's energy was really flagging by now, as I walked him back to the couch and laid him down to remove the plastic protectant. I re-bandaged him and dressed him in a T-shirt and pajama bottoms. I put his arm around my shoulder and walked him to the bed. He crawled into the clean, fresh sheets of his own bed for the first time in forty-five days. He was asleep before I brought the quilt up to his chin.

Harry had lost thirty-five to forty pounds while in the hospital. He had lost a lot of muscle and had become very weak. Once he got home he lost even more weight and became even weaker. Realize that while he was in the hospital, he received a bag of nutrients every day. Now at home, the only way to get nutrition into him was through his mouth. After so many days without food, his stomach capacity was minuscule. I would feed him a tablespoon of food every twenty minutes. Very gradually, the portions got larger, but it took many weeks for him to be able to tolerate even a small meal.

Just as my friend Terry said, I woke perhaps twenty times a night. Sometimes I would prop myself up on my elbow to watch Harry and listen to make sure he was still breathing. When he switched positions, I always woke up and would hold my breath until he settled into sleep again and I could relax knowing that he was okay.

Harry ties with his father for being the most social person I know. In the days after he came home, however, he did not want any visitors. He was so exhausted, so completely out of gas, he couldn't fathom summoning the energy to visit with family or friends, not even his parents.

Harry was determined to fight his exhaustion and lack of appetite, knowing that it was the quickest way back to recovery. In the first few days, it was everything he could do to go back and forth to the bathroom with his arm wrapped around my shoulder and navigate the stairs for those small portions of food. Then, he began adding steps each day to what he accomplished the day before. First it was five steps down the hall, then ten. Then, a walk to the front door, the next day, ten steps from the door. Within two weeks, he could walk to the edge of the cul-de-sac. A satisfying nap always followed his exercise and a routine developed that gradually increased his appetite, food capacity, stamina and strength. One only needed to watch him every day to realize that these were really tough days. But Harry never gave up, never complained and he soon began to actually feel like himself. I often marveled at his perseverance and fortitude, and those are my clearest memories of those days. I still marvel at what a huge effort it was for Harry to heal.

"Welcome home Harry! And I'm sure everyone in the house, including the dogs, are REALLY happy you finally took a shower."
~KW

"Welcome home, Harry! What a precious gift life is, and the love of friends and family! That love, and the enormous amount of prayers He received because of that love, have made this, and every single day going forward, just as special as the day before. I can't think of a better way to get well, than cuddling on the couch with the greatest, strongest, and most courageous woman I have had the luxury of observing. You and your family are so blessed, Harry! Best of luck to you, also, Harrison! The game of football is a 'walk-in-the-park' when compared to the courage, and fight, you have just conquered with your dad."
~MF

"Welcome home! What wonderful news! I'm so glad you are home—now, I can stop holding my breath."
~JD

"Dear Harry, Cathy and H Man,
WELCOME HOME HARRY! What wonderful news and a great way to end the evening! So glad that Harry is settling in and that the Whites are all together again under the same roof ... what a blessing. Looking forward to seeing Harry's beautiful smile, impeccable dress and perfect hair... :-). Enjoy this very beautiful weekend and happy, happy homecoming Harry!"
~KW

"What fabulous good news! Congrats to you, Harry, and here's to your heroic Cathy and Harrison. I've always known you were a good man, inside and out, but this is stupendous. My best wishes and prayers go with you, particularly now that the real work and reflection begin. God bless you, especially now

that you've gotten the hell out of that bed! I often sign off, as I will now, with these deeply felt words, never more to the point than for you, and us, today ... Be well!"
~BE

Saturday, September 5, 2009

A Day We Will Always Remember!

HE DID IT!!! Harry went to Harrison's first football game of his high school career!

It was just two weeks ago today that Harry told his surgeon that he wanted to be out of the hospital in time to go to Harrison's first football game. I can still remember the look that the doctor and I exchanged—a look that said "that is *highly* doubtful." Just a week ago today, Harry was still in CCU, recovering from having his abdomen closed the day before. Remarkable!

Scott (Batzi's husband) drove Batzi, Harry, and me to the game. The school had given us their blessing to pull our van up to the net at the back of the end zone. Harry was able to watch the entire game from the front seat. We were prepared, with an air-bed in the back of the van (which Harry never needed), pillows, and a cooler full of drinks and food.

Our Junior Varsity team won 41-0. The first score of the game was a touchdown pass to … *Harrison White*!! I can't begin to tell you how thrilled I was at that moment to have Harry watching the game! It was a dream come true. It is tradition, that after the game, the players kneel in front of the fans and sing the alma mater, standing up at the last line. This never fails to give me goose-bumps but it was especially beautiful to me today. After the boys finished that, they turned and began running down to us at the end zone. They stopped in front of the car, and lined up in formation to do the "Quick Drill." The Quick Drill is a precise performance of crisp, athletic discipline, and it is something that Harry loves to watch. The players gave a respectful display of admiration and support for the man who has coached many of these boys in flag football for the past four years. When the boys finished, Harry got out of the car, walked over to the net and put his hand up to meet the hands of the players and coaches.

I am so proud of Harry for his determination to be at today's game. He knew that the risk of going today would be increased pain and fatigue, but he chose to do it anyway. His discomfort and exhaustion have definitely increased tonight, but he says—

it is totally worth it! Today has been a very emotional, but extremely happy day—one that we will always remember.

This will be my last daily update. In a few days, I will let you know how Harry is progressing, but I think we can all be confident now that although the journey is not quite at an end—it is a much smoother road than it has been. Harry will take some time getting back to normal. Some doctors say that may be almost a year. But *we* all know it will be much sooner than that!

Thank you for traveling with us through these past forty-five incredible days. We couldn't have had this happy ending without your prayers. Your love and caring continue to overwhelm us.

There is a phrase that some of you have sent to me in the past month and a half—

"People will forget what you said, People will forget what you did, But people will never forget how you made them feel."

Thank you for making us feel so loved..... we will never forget it!

Harry, Cathy and Harrison White

Harry was so determined to be at that football game! Yet, he was so frail and feeling poorly—devoid of energy, nauseous, and in a lot of pain. I wasn't sure it was the wisest decision, but we made the most of the situation. Batzi and I were prepared for anything. I put an inflatable mattress in the back of the van, with blankets and pillows, should Harry need to lie down during the game. We had a cooler packed with easy-to-eat foods and liquids that we thought might help his energy—watermelon, yogurt, applesauce, gatorade. As it turned out, he consumed very little while we were at the game. The preparation to get to the car and the drive itself had further tired Harry and ruined what little appetite he did have. When I strapped him in to the front passenger seat, I could tell by the look on his face that we would be lucky to make it to the end of the game. We hadn't even left the house, but he already looked exhausted. The drive to school was painful, as it had been the day before when we drove home from the hospital. It was a relief to stop the car. Parking in the end zone was perfect! Harry could watch the entire game from the relative comfort and warmth of the car and could preserve his energy further by not getting out and trying to walk or socialize. Over the next couple of hours, I could see his energy draining even further. When the game ended, I was standing next to the open passenger window. The second it ended, Harry turned to me, with his eyes at half-mast and said, "We should go." The look on his face told me that he had nothing left and he desperately needed to go home to bed. He had used every bit of energy and fortitude to make it through the past two hours and he was done. I told him that I thought the team might come down to this end of the field to say hello and when I asked him if he could make it just a few more minutes, he said, "yes." I'm sure nobody realized how spent he was. When he got out of the car to go to the fence, I was completely amazed. My unending gratitude and love go out to our dear friend, Coach Welch. Knowing that it would be a highlight of Harry's life, and wanting to make the day especially wonderful for Harry, he, of course, called the play for the touchdown pass to go to Harrison. What a wonderfully loving gift Coach Welch gave to our family on this incredible, most memorable day!!

"Dear Harry, WELCOME HOME! As I read the account of Saturday's festivities, my eyes welled up with tears! I have

been so blessed to be a part of your family and to see how God brought the miracle of your recovery to reality that I will never forget going to my computer looking for the latest email to see your progress! Few people in life make such a real difference but you are a true exception. In most cases the "good guys" finish last but in your case you won the race! The backing of a loving wife, a wonderful son and a family that was there for you through every step of the way really shine through this trial. Take care, Harry and I will keep in touch. God Bless you and your family! Your friend forever.... "
~BJM

"Harry, The picture of you behind the net at the game says it all. There are not enough superlatives to describe the emotion that stirs in all of us. Cathy, with a huge lump in my throat, I say that all of us will miss your daily updates with all of your inspirational, positive energy. You helped us through a very trying episode and we will all forever be more thankful for what we have. And, Harrison ... You did exactly what you needed to do to make Saturday a magical day of miracles—TOUCHDOWN!!!!"
~NK

"Hi You Guys, Amazing, just absolutely amazing! I knew Harry could do it! Harrison, way to score that first touchdown—how cool is that!? I read this journal entry today out loud to my husband and I just cried with joy!!! I know that we may not see each other all the time anymore like we used to in Little League but I want you to know that you all have touched our lives so much by allowing us to share this journey with you. I will miss reading about Harry every day and I will be looking forward to hearing about his progress."
~LK

"It is totally surreal that Harrison made the first touchdown of the season in honor of his father, what a beautiful expression of love. I don't know what I will do without my nightly updates, but knowing Harry is on the mend makes it OK!

God Bless all the Whites for their journey and God Bless you, Harry and Harrison that life will only be beautiful from this moment on. Love you all,"
~JD

"What a most memorable day! It was totally fitting that H Man scored the first touchdown ... he knew how much it meant to have his dad with him at this game! Wow ... what a feeling that must have been! A definite sign of wonderful things ahead!"
~KW

"Way to go Harry! YOU also scored a touchdown!"
~FM

"All I can say is, praise the Lord. God has been involved in this miracle."
~LL

"Dear Harry, Cathy & Harrison,
I got the warm and happy chills and a tear of joy when I read Cathy's last entry and saw the picture which showed an image I'll never forget; Harry at Harrison's first football game!!! Wow! What a cool tribute those boys gave Harry! That must have really felt good to experience!!! Harrison, you must have been so very proud (once again) of your wonderful father and mother! I'm tremendously happy for all of you and I want you to know that I've been so inspired by your courage and sense of life! Yours is a life well lived."
~KR

"I just read the journal entry from Saturday. What a winning day!! Not only did you see Harrison in his big moment, but he was able to see you, Harry, in yours! I keep thinking about just a month ago ... how tenuous each day was, yet Saturday, you were at the field watching your son play football. It's all so incredibly surreal! Since you are 'on the road to recovery,' 'may the road rise to meet you ... may the wind be

always at your back and may God hold you (just as He has been) in the palm of His hand!'''
~JH

"A bit from a favorite song:

'I've heard it said that people come into our lives for a reason,
Bringing something we must learn,
And we are led to those who help us most to grow
If we let them, and we help them in return
Well, I don't know if I believe that's true,
But I know that I'm who I am today because I knew you
Like a comet pulled from orbit as it passes the sun,
Like a stream that meets a boulder halfway through the wood,
Who can say if I've been changed for the better
(I do believe I have been changed for the better)
But, because I knew you, I have been changed for good.'
("For Good" Written by Stephen Schwartz)

I have been changed.... Witnessing your love for each other through Cathy's most painful, then uplifting journals. Through Harry's strength, absolute determination and passion for life. Through Harrison's bravery and inspiration to his loving father. Through the love and support of family and friends witnessed every day in this guestbook. I know the journey is not quite over yet. But I hope the memories of the difficulty and pain of these past long weeks will soon fade and be replaced by beautiful memories of the good times ahead. Harrison's football game is a fabulous start!
I don't mind crying happy tears at all! I love you,"
~CP

"Dear Harry, I can't tell you how much I have been touched by this life changing experience you have been on, mostly by your beautiful Cathy's daily words and strength. Even though you have not seen us, we have been on this journey with you, praying, always looking forward to the next journal update and hearing about your progress and community

happenings. It truly is amazing to see such devotion shine when situations arise."
~SG

"There are memories and then there are MEMORIES!!!!!! Today was the latter."
~MD

Wednesday, September 9, 2009

31 Years Ago Today ...

This is our 31st wedding anniversary. And, yes, this is the *happiest anniversary we have ever had*!! When I think that just five weeks ago, I feared becoming a widow, and now I am looking forward to dozens more anniversary celebrations—it's an answer to my prayers.

Today is very different from our usual way of celebrating our anniversary. We traditionally go on a three-to-four-day romantic getaway. (We have postponed the trip and will go right at the thirty-one-and-a-*half*-year mark.) But these last few days have been as sweet and bonding as any trip we've ever been on. Some of you who have gone through an illness and recovery process like ours have told me that it changed your relationship for the better. We have always had a great relationship, and I didn't think it could get much better. But it is happening. I feel it already, and I know that becoming even closer will continue as we face together the challenges of the next few months. It's one of the many beautiful blessings that have come out of these disastrous weeks.

I know you are anxious to hear how Harry is doing! He is doing better, improving by small steps each day. He LOVES being home. He appreciates every simple thing that most of us take for granted—fresh air, a shower, peace and quiet when he wants it, his own bed and pillow, soft sheets, tasty, healthy food, and nobody asking to take his vitals in the middle of the night!!

Harry's appetite and stomach capacity have increased, so he is really beginning to benefit from good nutrition. He is getting slightly stronger every day. He can go up and down the stairs (although he needs a big rest between treks), and walks about five times per day around our cul-de-sac. Each trip exhausts him, but he does it and enjoys the clean air and warm sun. When I think about where he was just a week ago—I am so proud of the progress he's made.

We aren't yet seeing visitors, because the things that are the biggest challenge for Harry right now are fatigue, pain and low energy, and visiting is still a bit much for him. Harry has lost a lot of weight, and to call him 'frail' is pretty accurate. To illustrate how tired he gets—on Sunday, he asked me to cut his hair. While cutting his hair, we had to do it in three stages, because it was too tiring and uncomfortable for him to sit there for twenty to thirty minutes.

Harry has five doctor's appointments in the next two weeks. On Friday, half of the metal staples will be removed from his stomach 'zipper.' He also has physical therapy at the house three times per week. His days are a series of rests, a bit of exercise, and small meals. He still has a long way to go before resuming normal activity, but I can see a difference already in his recovery. I know it's not easy for him, but he doesn't complain—he just gets the job done.

A few days ago, I showed Harry his CaringBridge website. I started with the first day's entry, then read all of the emails that came in that day, and told him who called. Then, we went on to the next entry, and did the same. We will keep going until he has heard every last word you've written to and about him! We both love this part of our day. I think this is a highlight of these days of recovery for Harry. He is so amazed and touched at the things you have said. Often, he'll say, "That's just beautiful!", and sometimes he will say, "I had no idea they felt that way." I have no doubt that your loving words are helping him heal. Thank you for that! Cathy & Harry

*"HAPPY ANNIVERSARY!!! Wow! All four of my marriages
only total twenty-nine wonderful years!"*
~BJM

*"WOW ... another inspiring read from my favorite author!
Happy, happy anniversary to both of you!! It's been thirty-one
years, and the warmth in your smiles has not dampened over
the years. :) I've missed the Whites in my nightly routine;
your words are a wonderful reminder of how precious life
is and how the simplest things are indeed a gift. I shake
my head in amazement and admiration as I reflect back on
your journey ... your journals and words, Cathy, will make an
incredible book, providing words of inspiration and strength
to those seeking comfort and compassion. I've discovered
that a successful life is not measured by the riches in 'things,'
but by the richness in knowing that you have made a positive
impact in people's lives. It seems that part of the purpose of
your hardship will be to continue to 'positively affect' people
for years beyond even yours. What a great honor!! Continue
your road to health and recovery, Harry. So many friends are
rooting for you!!"*
~CG

*"HAPPY ANNIVERSARY... HAPPY ANNIVERSARY...
HAPPY ANNIVERSARY ... HAAAAPPPPY ANNI-
VERSARY! (happy, happy, happy, happy, happy anniversary
and so the song goes) Lucky for you both there is no volume
... as my family says my voice can bring down the best of
celebrations. I just come back with ... the Lord says to make a
joyful noise ... AND I AM JOYFUL ;) !!!"*
~JH

*"Happy 31st Wedding Anniversary!!! What a wonderful
blessing that you are able to share your special day together
at home. You all have been through so much but God continues
to bless you. Yes, this journey will continue to bring you closer
together. It is amazing how God does this for us—Cathy, you
mentioned Harry being 'frail'—I can't even imagine that!!*

Harry, I know you will not be that way long. You have lots of perseverance, a passion for life, and it shows in all ways. Cathy, you too, you never give up. I am confident you will nurse Harry back to health in short order. Thank you for being such an inspiration to all of us out here! A verse ... I carry with me ... Philippians 4:6–7 ... Be anxious for nothing, but in everything by prayer and supplication, with thanksgiving, let your requests be known to God; and the peace of God, which surpasses all understanding, will guard your hearts and minds through Christ Jesus.' May you have a wonderful day together and always!"
~CS

"Being HOME must be the greatest romantic get-away gift for both of you! Enjoy— :-)"
~VF

"Happy Anniversary, Harry and Cathy!! This will, without a doubt be the happiest, most memorable one yet. Gotta love that it is 09/09/09!!"
~AG

"'There are those whose lives affect all others around them, quietly touching one heart, who in turn, touches another, reaching out to ends further than they would ever know.'
-William Bradfield
This says it perfectly!"
~BH

Wednesday, September 16, 2009

Better and Better by the Day

Harry is doing better each day. Sometimes the forward progress is minor, sometimes better than expected. Using the days of the week for comparison shows me how much progress he is actually making. When he came home on September 4th, he was extremely exhausted from just getting to the car in a wheelchair and the one-way car ride to our house. A week later, when I drove him to get half of his stitches out, he tolerated the drive in both directions, and was able to walk to and from the doctor's office from the parking lot—no wheelchair necessary. Remember the Sunday where he couldn't sit up for a haircut? A week later found him walking down the street—to eight houses away from ours!

Harry's appetite is good, and he can eat just about anything now that sounds good. He needs to gain weight (a position we all wish we shared!), as he is still very thin. But he is working on it by eating healthy foods, resting and exercising.

This week is busy with appointments—one every day. Today, Harry had blood drawn at the lab, and we are anxious to find out how the kidney and liver functions are doing. I am going to guess that the kidneys are back to normal, and that liver function is close. There is still some residual yellow to his skin, and some in the whites of his eyes. Considering that the whites of his eyes were once the yellow of a sunflower, I'd say he has come a long way!

Yesterday, Harry's visit to his cardiologist went really well. His EKG was perfect. His blood pressure, that I have been taking since his arrival home, has averaged 120/75. The cardiologist told him, in his beautiful South African accent, "Harry, mate, your ticker is the strongest part of your body!!"

Fatigue is Harry's biggest challenge, as it has been since we arrived home. He is sleeping well at night now, and naps a few times throughout the day. I'm sure he wishes he had more energy, but resting is the best thing that he can do for himself. When we talk about everything that his body has endured, it reminds us both that the road to complete recovery will understandably be a long one.

And, yes—Harry saw Harrison's second football game! The school was kind enough to once again grant us access to the end zone, because Harry would not have been able to sit in a wheelchair in the stands through the entire game. No touchdowns this time, but Harrison and his teammates played a great game, beating probably one of the best opponents all year, 28-14. On offense, H plays slot receiver and back-up quarterback. On defense, he plays outside linebacker, and on special teams, he is the PAT holder. He saw a lot of action on defense this week.

During the game, several people came by to visit Harry in the end zone. It was—quite emotional at times. And, something I will never forget. At half-time, the JV cheerleaders came by to say hello to Dr. White (tonight's photo). Many of their parents are dear friends of ours, and they were so sweet and respectful to Harry—it brought a huge lump to my throat. *Thank you, JV Cheer!! XO*

What a difference for Harry this past weekend at the game. That comparison of the week before showed me how much he has accomplished in seven short days. He looked, felt, and moved better at Saturday's game. Give him a few more weeks, and he will be getting closer and closer to feeling himself.

Every day, we are still enjoying our reading together of Harry's days in the hospital, and your corresponding emails, guestbook entries, cards, and phone messages. We read *every* word together, and I can't tell you how delightful it's been.

There are so many ancillary stories that I can now tell Harry along with the daily entries. I tell Harry about every single thing that you brought to the hospital—food, coffee, bottled waters, flowers, magazines, cards, pictures, and room decorations.

I tell Harry about all the people who came to visit him, or me, or his family—some even from out of town, and out of state. I've told him that of all the people that came to see him while he was in the hospital, three fourths of the men ... *cried* when they saw him.

Harry's cousin, Luke, came one day from Stockton, to pray over him. Luke is an imposing figure, at 6'8", in his Greek

Orthodox Priest ensemble and black beard. You should have seen everyone double-take as he passed them in the halls of CICU! I'm sure everyone expected that he was entering Harry's room to give him last rites—their expressions told me so! Humorous now—not so funny then!

Quite often in the emails to me in those early days, many of you would say, "Please give Harry a kiss for us." One time, when I read this line, I looked up to see Harry puckering his lips. (You can see it, can't you?) Of course, I leaned over to kiss him! Now, not a request for a kiss goes unanswered. When I have read five or six emails without a kiss request, Harry will say, "Didn't they ask you to give me a kiss? I'm sure they would have wanted you to give me a kiss!" He *is* getting better, isn't he?!?!

XO,
Cathy and Harry

"Yes, Cathy ... please give Harry ANOTHER and ANOTHER kiss from us. :-)
Love you, dear ones,"
~MF

"The sweetness of your kisses for each other brings tears to my eyes. God bless you both. Harry, keep up the great work ... one step at a time, one day at a time."
~MK

"Harry, You sly little devil, you! We get it now— 'stomach staples'— 'lost 35-40 pounds'—heart attack schmart attack, you had a 'tummy tuck' and you look FANTASTIC! PS ... It's our secret! Get well soon!"
~KG

Tuesday, September 22, 2009

Moving Toward A Full Recovery

Last week was one of great progress for Harry. He completed four doctors' check-ups last week, and all are very pleased with his progress. On Thursday, the last thirty of the fifty-eight metal staples were removed from his abdomen, as was the fifteen-inch drain that was draining the incision that runs from mid-chest to pelvis. He feels markedly better now that all the hardware is out of his body. We saw the kidney doctor on Friday, who gave him a clean bill of health for the kidneys—*function is perfectly normal now!* The liver numbers are still slightly above normal, but continuing to inch downward—bilirubin is now 2.9 (was 20 at one point), and normal is about 0.7.

Dr. Frank is an internist with a specialty in infectious diseases. He saw Harry every day while at the hospital, sometimes twice a day, as infection from the many possible sources (IV lines, incision, drain, dialysis port, etc.) was the biggest risk over the last couple of weeks in the hospital. He is the one who discovered and treated Harry's gnarly intestinal infection. He was so thrilled to see how much better Harry looked and to track his blood work success. At the end of the exam, Dr. Frank looked at me and smiled, and said, "It was a good save, wasn't it?" Oh ...YES ... it was a good save!!! When we left the office, Dr. Frank gave us both big hugs. His genuine happiness over Harry's survival and complete return to health was so evident, so bonding with us, and I know we will never forget him.

Nor will we ever forget our other wonderful doctors, nurses, therapists, and assistants—the team that banded together to do their best to help Harry not just survive, but survive without any permanent damage. At this point, it looks like that is the case. Every system of his body is expected to eventually return to normal. Another miracle ...

A little side note here for the students of Kate's class: Thank you for following Dr. White's journey! As future doctors, nurses, therapists and medical technicians, you could not have a better example to follow than the personnel at the hospital that took care of Dr. White. Always remember that you can choose to be a good doctor, or a great one. A great doctor fully engages in the challenges of treating all aspects of each individual patient. Smart medical personnel know that the best success is reached by addressing not just the body, its symptoms and test results. The remarkable doctors, nurses and techs make a connection with their patients—treating them respectfully as the human beings they are. They understand the importance of compassion, a kind word, a shared laugh. They communicate well and make their patients feel special—almost like a family member. They listen to the needs of the patient, and care for the family, too. They feed the soul and the spirit, while treating the body. That's what Harry's medical team did for him!! There is no doubt that their special care not only saved his life, but sped his recovery, and spared him from permanent damage.

Overall, Harry is feeling better. His appetite is picking up, and he can walk for about ten to fifteen minutes at a time now. He does that several times per day. He still sleeps and rests a lot—fatigue gets ahold of him off and on throughout the day, but that is certainly to be expected. He is still very thin, and a bit gaunt, especially since his skin is still a little yellow. But he looks much better than he did when he came home two weeks ago!! He's definitely on the mend!!

We continue to enjoy reading the journal entries and accompanying emails and guestbook entries every day. Each day's reading prompts a story or two (or five or six!) that cause Harry to shake his head in disbelief. He is still shocked by the severity of his situation—still a bit disbelieving that this all happened to him. And, he is touchingly surprised at the outpouring of love and admiration for him. Many of your notes bring us both to tears. The tissue is always within reach!

I don't think we will ever know how far reaching the prayers and positive thoughts for us were. We have heard from many strangers, and from friends and supporters as far away as Thailand, Nairobi and Panama. It worked, our friends! The powerful prayers, the positive thoughts ... that and a great team of medical personnel—it worked! It gave us the happy ending for which we all fervently prayed!
Harry and Cathy

"I have been heavily impacted by your miracle recovery, Harry, and Cathy's remarkable showing of strength as your wife. WOW, what an example you two have set, and what a story you have! I read every word you wrote every day, Cathy, and have prayed unceasingly. The lives you both have touched and will continue to touch are numerous and uncountable in human terms. Only our Lord knows the details ... God is so good. The depth of my emotions (both high and low) has been an incredible roller coaster ride that I wouldn't trade for anything. I'm proud to be your friend, and proud to have partnered in prayer for you and your family (and that, of course, goes for my hubby, too). We look forward to many good times together as you get closer and closer to full recovery."
~RT

"I just finished reading your entire journal and can't believe the miracle that has taken place. After my many years of doing bedside care, I have seen several, but never one involving multiple organ shutdown!!! God has certainly honored all those prayers for you and favorably looked down on all the love and admiration so many have for you!"
~CH

"Dear Harry, It is always hard to believe when such a young and vibrant person is affected by near tragedy. It just can't be possible. But thankfully, your return to health is an inspiration as your positive attitude and outlook in life has always been a treat for anyone who has ever had the privilege to know you or meet you. Though we only ran into each other infrequently, you were always jovial, smiling and full of energy. You are a great example of how with a positive outlook, no matter what curves life throws you, you can successfully impact your ability to face adversity."
~TD

Monday, October 5, 2009

The Miracle Man Turns 60 on Thursday!

October 8, 2009—Harry White's 60th Birthday

It's a milestone that many thought Harry would never reach. Against all odds, he is here to celebrate his 60th birthday!

We were just beginning to plan a birthday party for Harry when he had his "issues." We will still do that party, but it will need to be postponed until sometime after the first of the year. The day itself will be no less happy than if we were having the bash of the century!

Harry is improving by the day. Some days are better than others, but overall, he is steadily gaining strength and stamina. He is eating better and walking farther each day. He still struggles with fatigue, but one of his doctors told him that he will probably deal with that for two more months. By the first part of December, he should be feeling more energetic and more like himself.

I wish you could see the expressions on the faces of friends when they see Harry for the first time since his release from the hospital. It is a thing of beauty, and something I am enjoying so much right now. It's rather difficult to describe, but everyone shares this expression. There is relief, of course, because there is something reassuring about actually seeing Harry with one's own eyes. Then, the relief is replaced by pure joy. And, finally, there is a bit of reverence, as if each person that sees him appreciates the witnessing of the miracle of his survival.

One of Harry's goals last week was to make it to Back to School Night on September 29th. He didn't feel particularly well that day, but it was very important to him to be at the first BtS Night of Harrison's high school years, so he went. His presence was not expected, so it was a pleasant surprise for many. There were lots of happy smiles, many careful hugs, and a few tears.

Before the evening started, I told our headmaster how much we appreciate everything that the school community did and continues to do to help us. The warmth, caring and assistance from our school community have been *second to none*, and I wouldn't want to imagine how we would have made it through without them. Once he welcomed everyone, he paid a beautiful, touching tribute to Harry. He thanked the parents and faculty on our behalf, and Harry enjoyed a wonderful, lengthy ovation. It was incredibly touching, very emotional—and a moment neither of us will ever forget.

On Friday, September 26th, Harry saw his surgeon, who was so pleased with his progress, that he doesn't need to see him again for a month. He agreed with Dr. Frank's assessment that "this was a good save." He told us that in his experience, complete multi-system organ failure, such as Harry had, has a mortality rate of 98 percent—that 98 percent of patients with complete organ failure do not live. Since that day, our various friends in the medical field have admitted to us that they feared that Harry had no chance of survival, given what he had been through, and knowing what they know from years of experience.

Once Harry regained consciousness, Bill and Kathi returned to California from Colorado for a couple of days to visit. During the visit, Bill and Harry were talking about what a miracle Harry's survival is, and how wonderful it is for Harry to be given a second chance. To that Harry replied, "I'm going to do something with my life, Bill." That comment made me smile.

This from a man who has already done so much? He has given thousands of patients beautiful smiles to enjoy for the rest of their lives. He has coached dozens of athletes in a manner that would make John Wooden proud. He is a wonderful father and husband, a loving, attentive son and brother, and a great friend. He treats everyone—family, friends and strangers—with compassion, gracious friendliness and respect. And, yet, he says that he is going to do something with his life!?! I have no doubt that if anyone will make the most of a second chance at life, it will be Harry White.

I think it's quite possible that ... the best is yet to be. I can't wait to see what the future brings!

Happy Birthday, Miracle Man!!!
I love you, Cat

"Harry, I was so thrilled to see you at back-to-school night. I gave my husband so much grief for not being able to make it, I told him ... even Harry was there after everything he's been through!"
~LF

"Harry and Cathy, Reading your journal has been inspirational for us. We are so grateful for Harry's recovery. Cathy, your love, strength and commitment toward Harry is what got him through this ... I have no doubt. I hug my husband a little harder every night when he walks through the door. Life is to be cherished and I have no doubt not a day will go by that you three will not appreciate every moment. Harry, your recovery has been especially poignant for my husband, having lost his father when he was nine. He always asks how you are doing, and is overjoyed at the outcome. We look forward to reading your journal until we read that you are 100 percent, no matter how long it may take. Health and love to all,
P.S. Nobody should look that good after what you have been through. What is that all about!?!?!?"
~KB

"Well, I thought I was done crying while reading these journal entries, but Cath, you did it again!! HAPPY, HAPPY BIRTHDAY HARRY from Sydney, Australia! I'm so happy for your continued recovery and strength and I can't wait to hear 'what you're going to do with your life!!!' Lots of love,"
~NK

"As I was sharing with my son that your birthday is on Thursday and that you will be sixty years old ... he said ... 'Sixty? ... Dr. White? ... 60?'!!!! I had to let him read it for himself as he thought I was crazy!!! I have to agree with him! Not that I'm crazy!... but that the number doesn't fit with your youthful look ... youthful outlook ... and your youthful zest for life! What a gift this birthday is and what a gift you are. All of our best birthday wishes ... from the bottom of our hearts!"
~JM

"I am not surprised by your remarkable recovery ... Dr. White, you have always inspired me to be not only good ... but better!! And it is no wonder that a class act like you would show not only the doctors ... but the world what you are made of!! You, Cathy and Harrison will always have a part of my heart."
~AB

"I am relieved that you are with us and you 'keep on truckin'.' Besides, these messages won't be necessary for much longer and I, poor, balding curmudgeon that I am, won't have to listen to another song of praise and delight for your damned hair!"
~BE

"Dr White, What is a Gentleman? That's a word you don't hear much anymore. It brings to mind a certain kind of man, who's thoughtful, caring, considerate and all too uncommon these days. But that's exactly who you are. You're a rare and special man who deserves the best. Happy Birthday!"
~RR

"Hello Harry, You're a very blessed man with a wonderful and loving family and friends, but no one deserves and has earned the love and friendships more than you. Over the years you have been a great husband, father and friend to many. I am very proud to call you a friend. Wishing you many happy years! Take care, Harry,"
~CD

Tuesday, November 24, 2009

Two days before Thanksgiving

Visiting the Hospital

It was four months ago this week that Harry was first admitted to the hospital. In those four months, he went from health to the brink of death and back. It seemed a fitting day to do something special ... so we visited the staff at the hospital, because we wanted to say a few thank yous. Harry also was anxious to see his Cardiac Intensive Care room, as his memories of it were almost non-existent. What an emotional day it turned out to be!

Before I describe the day, I will answer the question that everyone still asks. *How is Harry doing?* Once again, he is surprising us all. He is doing so well!! To see him now, you wouldn't know he had been sick. His blood test from ten days ago shows that everything is back to normal—kidneys and liver and even PSA are better than ever! He has put on a few pounds and his color looks great. There is still some pain and discomfort in the abdomen, but the incision has healed well and is even beginning to soften and fade a bit. Harry is eating well, sleeping less, and gradually increasing his exercise. Yesterday, he went for a seven mile walk. Yep—seven miles!! Life is slowly returning to normal, something I never dreamt would happen this soon. Harry is amazing—the way he has handled his recovery is *inspirational.*

Our trip to the hospital evoked a wide range of emotions—relief, dread, sadness, hope, happiness, fear, and comfortable and uncomfortable familiarity. From the moment we pulled into the parking structure, our emotions were on red-alert. I took Harry in through the main entrance, pointing out the different places where family and friends had eaten, the surgery waiting room, the bank of elevators that became as familiar to me as a second home. I showed him where I sat in the waiting area the first night, speaking with his doctors, and I showed him the beautiful view from the room where the Zacharys brought me dinner one night. All of this was unfamiliar to Harry.

Then, we stepped into CCU, and several nurses turned to

look at us. First, they glanced at me with easy recognition and then as their gazes turned to Harry, recognition dawned and the expressions on their faces were rapturous. It was such a beautiful sight, one I will never, ever forget. The nurses surrounded us with hugs and tears. As we walked around, we saw more and more nurses, some of our doctors, some respiratory therapists and technicians. There were at least thirty people that gave us hugs, accepted our thanks, and thanked us in return for coming by. Nobody could believe how good Harry looks! At one point, when Harry wondered if we would run into any of the dialysis nurses, I looked down the hall to see Britanny, the dialysis nurse that took care of Harry the first night. The mental vision of the look on her face when she recognized us brings tears to my eyes as I type this. She slowly stood up and said, "Oh, my God! I can't believe it! How wonderful you look. You're a walking miracle, Dr. White!"

The tour of CCU did bring back some memories for Harry. He spent thirteen days in Room 20, which he didn't remember well, but he spent the night after the abdominal closing surgery in Room 14, and that one he remembered better. After leaving the fourth floor, we went to the sixth floor, where he had spent eleven days in two separate rooms. His memories were much clearer here. Stepping into the waiting room made his stomach drop, as this was the turn-around spot for his walks, and he associated that location with how terrible he felt during those first walks. Then, happier memories took over as we saw more and more nurses and technicians who were thrilled to see The Miracle Man.

It seems apropos that we visited the hospital to say our thank yous during Thanksgiving week. We were so appreciative of the opportunity to show the staff the result of their hard work and fervent efforts. Harry's health issues challenged them, and they more than met the challenge. We are especially grateful to them and have them in our Thanksgiving thoughts and prayers.

We have you, too, our friends and family, in our thoughts this weekend. We are truly blessed to call you our friends.

Happy Thanksgiving,
Harry, Cathy and Harrison

There were so many side stories that I didn't have time to include in my daily postings. This is, without a doubt, one of my favorites....

Harry and I had been talking for a couple of weeks about going back to the hospital to thank the staff members there. He also wanted to see where he had been, because his memory of the rooms and the people was minimal. We decided the perfect time for that was around Thanksgiving. On the Tuesday before Thanksgiving, we visited. We brought a flower arrangement with us and walked to the entry door of the ICU. As I had done what seemed 1,000 times before, I pushed the entry button. A nurse's voice came back and I told her who I was and that we wanted to come in to thank everyone.

As we entered and staff members looked over at us, I could see recognition when they saw me and ran over to us. Everyone smiled and was welcoming. Then, their eyes would switch to Harry and their jaws would drop open. Before we knew it, we were surrounded by nurses, orderlies and doctors. There were tears and many exclamations of "I can't believe it!"

The staff members thanked US, for coming back to show them the results of their efforts—a patient who had survived against all odds, thanks to their care and dedication. So often, care givers never know what happens to the patients after they leave the ICU. As we walked around, more and more familiar faces greeted us with big smiles and hugs. I pointed out to Harry the various rooms in which he had stayed. As we turned a corner, we saw Harry's infectious disease specialist, Dr. Frank, in the hallway (the one that called this "a good save"). He was thrilled to see us and to see how well Harry was doing. He greeted us warmly and told Harry that he looked even better than he had on his post-hospital release appointment. We chatted for a few minutes and then he pulled us aside to discuss a situation with a patient he currently had in ICU.

His patient, Hank, had been in ICU for about three months, with kidney failure and several other serious issues. He was very ill and emotionally ready to give up his fight for survival. He asked if we would be willing to speak with Hank and his wife and without hesitation, we agreed.

Dr. Frank brought Hank's wife out into the hallway to meet with us and to tell her that he wanted Harry to talk to Hank. He explained that Harry had left the ICU just ten weeks earlier and that while he was in the hospital, he was in worse shape than Hank, with a lower percentage of survival. She was exhausted, afraid and broke into tears saying, "He's ready to give up."

We entered Hank's room and Dr. Frank introduced us and explained Harry's situation to Hank. He then left us to chat and Hank and Harry had a wonderful conversation about their professions. As a football coach, some of Hank's players had also been patients of Harry's.

After a while, Harry stressed to Hank that he just could not give up. He pointed to a photo on the wall of Hank's young granddaughter and implored him to survive for her as well as for his other family members. Harry acknowledged Hank's wife and daughter, standing by the bed in tears. He told him if HE could survive, Hank could do it. Harry said, "You've got to get up and move and you've got to eat. It will be the hardest thing you've ever done. I know you don't want to do it and you don't have the physical or emotional strength. But you've got to do it for your family. Today, just take one or two steps down the hall, then tomorrow take five, then the next day take ten. It will take a long time, but gradually, your strength will return as will your appetite and your will to live."

We left Hank's room and the hospital in a blur of tears. It had been an emotional, but wonderful day. As we were driving home, Harry commented on how terrible Hank looked. He was drawn, painfully thin, yellow, gaunt and unhealthy looking. I laughed and said, "You looked EXACTLY like that!" He was shocked and said, "NO! That bad?"

Yes, indeed, he had looked that bad.

Early the next afternoon, we received a phone call from our friend Dana. Dana had been taking a golf lesson from her instructor, Geoff. Geoff's father had been extremely ill and Dana was afraid to ask him about his dad because she feared maybe he had passed away. But she did ask him and he stopped and looked at her and said, "It's the weirdest thing, Dana. For the last several days, we have been so sure that he was giving up the fight. We all think he was just hours away from giving in. But yesterday, a man and his wife came to see my dad and the man had been more sick than my dad. He survived and is doing really well. His words inspired my dad and he ended up having the best evening that he's had in weeks. He got out of bed and walked for a little bit and ate something and then said he slept better than he has in a long time. My mom is so relieved—she says she can see the spark of the will to live back in my dad's eyes. Dana told Geoff that she was happy that his dad was doing better. She explained that her friend, Harry, had been gravely ill for a long time and he survived, thanks to the great team at the hospital! Geoff's eyes widened and he slowly turned to Dana asking, "What's Harry's last name?" When Dana told him, "Dr. White," he took a deep, shaky breath and said, "That's the guy who visited my dad yesterday.... My mom says it's divine intervention."

From Hank's wife in February of 2010 …
"Your encouragement was such a gift to all of us that day you spent some time talking with Hank in November. To see you standing there, looking so wonderful, truly gave us all hope. You told him that at some point 'all' would come together and he would move forward rapidly. Hank appreciated your phone call the week of December 1st. He left the

hospital on December the 4th, after three plus months in the CardioVascular Intensive Care Unit, then went to acute rehab. The progress you spoke about started immediately. After about a week, I heard him tell a therapist that Dr. Harry White told me this would happen and shared what you had said to him. It was quite the moment. He was there for seventeen days; he came home December 23rd ... just in time for Christmas. He continues to progress each day. Walking with a cane now, eating all foods, jaundice nearly gone. Your inspiration has been crucial to our whole family. For you to have shown up at the hospital at such a critical time for Hank is overwhelming ... Divine intervention we think. We hope you are doing very well. We cannot thank you enough."
Love, Leslie

"I am so glad you went back to the hospital to see all of the dedicated, professional nurses and docs who helped take care of Harry. It must have melted their hearts to see him looking so handsome and healthy. Going back to say thank you means a lot to them, and it was so wonderful (but not surprising) of you to be so thoughtful. I am sure that returning was a HUGE and very emotional step. It holds so many pivotal moments for you ... where Harry almost lost his life and where it was saved. It is amazing how seeing the people and environment instantly takes you back to the time you 'lived' there. I really admire you both for going back even though you knew it would be difficult. I have wanted for a long time now to go back to the hospital where my son spent the last year and a half of his life battling leukemia. I grew to love and admire the people who were trying to save my son. They became like family. I can't even think of going back to where he suffered and died without feeling ill. But I really want and need to someday. I will think of you and the strength it took when I do return."
~SB

son for the season ... This community was rocked
ef four months ago. We are all thankful for your
ry. Your family continues to set the standard for giving

o wonderful to hear from you! It has been so inspirational
any of us who've had health challenges of our own, to hear
our miraculous story. I think outcomes like this give doctors
hope and inspiration, too, and remind us all that no matter
what the 'numbers' and 'statistics' say, there is an element in
healing that is spiritual and unpredictable. Have a wonderful
Thanksgiving and hope to see you soon."
~SC

"Dear Harry, Cathy and Harrison,
Thank you for your Thanksgiving message. Wow, what an
incredibly powerful day for you and your family. You truly
are the Miracle Man! We have kept you in our thoughts
and prayers and are thankful to hear that your recovery is
progressing so nicely. I never doubted for one minute that
you would fight this. I am just still in awe of the journey you
endured and the way you and your family faced each day. I
know this holiday season will be so wonderful for everyone
who loves you—having you healthy and happy is the biggest
blessing we have seen in many years. God Bless you and
Happy Holidays!"
~AD

"Seeing you all Saturday night, Harry was the same guy I
knew slightly at Stanford. I know he and you all are closer
to your God than most of us, and for that I envy you. No
one should go through what you did, but the outcome was a
miracle, and we need more of those."
~VF

March 25, 2010

On the Home Stretch

It's been over three months since our last update. And, in that time, Harry has gone from looking like someone who is "recovering from something" to looking like himself.

Harry is now doing really well. He looks and feels great—maybe even better than before his summer adventure. All of his systems are working within normal limits, and it shows in his color, energy and vitality. The only thing still not 100 percent is the abdomen. Regaining the abdominal muscle strength will still take some time, and there are areas of inflammation, tenderness, and swelling still present. We have been told it may be over a year before that is normal again. But, for the abdomen to be the only issue just eight months after complete organ failure, much progress has been made, and I'd say that Harry has done a remarkable job in regaining his health.

I'm proud of Harry for his commitment and willpower in doing what has been necessary to get himself so healthy to this point. He has put himself on a rigorous exercise program (taking a spin class twice a week, among other things!). He has rebuilt much of the muscle mass that was lost from forty-four days on his back in the hospital. He has been gradually weaning himself off of the various medications needed immediately after being released from the hospital, as they all have negative side effects to some extent. He has been able to eliminate the need for most of them, will eventually not take any at all, and has replaced some with natural, healthier supplements, a great diet, and effective exercise.

In November, Harry began experiencing some periodic chest pain. It was usually in the middle of the night, and lasted only about an hour or two. It occurred only sporadically. The second occurrence was while we were in the town of Bishop, a small, isolated town near the base of Mammoth Mountain in the foothills of the Sierra Nevada range. It is 315 miles from where we live! We were there for the weekend to watch Harrison and his teammates play their semi-final game of the football CIF championship. At 3:00 in the morning, waiting for the pain to subside, Harry and I looked at each other and didn't need to say a word to know that we were thinking the same thing … "Good Lord, we are in the middle of *nowhere*!!! Our wonderful cardiologist is 315 miles away." Luckily, the pain eased after about two hours.

Needless to say, as soon as we returned from Bishop, Harry went to see his cardiologist. He had an EKG and a cardiac nuclear stress test. He passed both with flying colors. The cardiologist told us that if one didn't know what had happened to Harry, it would be absolutely impossible to tell from the stress test. He said that his heart looks amazingly strong and healthy— as if nothing untoward had ever happened.

After a couple more months of tests, the use of sublingual nitroglycerin when the pain occurred, and a journal kept by Harry of his chest pain, our astute cardiologist told Harry that he thought he had a condition called Prinzmetal Angina. With Prinzmetal, there is a spasm of the coronary artery, with sudden tightening of the muscles of the walls of the arteries in the heart. When this occurs, the arteries narrow and prevent blood flow to the heart. This looks and feels like a blockage. Since this diagnosis, Harry has used sublingual nitroglycerine whenever he experiences these symptoms and he feels normal within minutes. At the time of this writing, Harry's heart continues to be monitored and continues to be healthy, without blockages. The Prinzmetal condition responds extremely well to the nitroglycerin and the occurrences are less and less with time and a healthy lifestyle.

Around this same time, our doctor ran tests on Harry that showed his digestive 'good-bacteria' balance was unusually low, probably due to being on antibiotics for four months. This imbalance can lead to several inflammation issues, so to treat the condition, Harry took a temporary dose of medication and probiotics, and he then went on a specialized month-long yeast-free diet. Right about three weeks into the diet, I noticed a *huge* difference in the way Harry looked. For the first time since July 23rd, he looked truly healthy, *all day long, every day*. He began to feel it, also—his energy, vitality, and comfort was beginning to feel normal. I can't tell you what a relief it was to see him looking so well.

The months that have passed have given me the chance to reflect on how grateful I am to everyone who helped us through last summer's ordeal. Instead of that gratitude fading with time, it has actually gotten stronger. I know I have said it before, but THANK YOU!!! I don't know how families make it through crises when they have no one around to help them!

I'd like to thank my parents and my brother, who did everything for us at home, so that I didn't come back from the hospital to a long list of household chores. They fed and walked the dogs, cooked meals, drove Harrison to and from football practice, did grocery shopping and errands, washed our cars, took our cars in for service, watered plants, and took care of laundry. It was such a relief to not have to worry about where to find the time for those necessary chores, and I don't know what I would have done without their help!

As I think now of my mom's thoughtful gesture when she did all my chores and laid out my nightgown on the bed that evening of August 15, I realize that she had done what so many of you were wanting to do for us. She wanted to do *something*, any little thing, to just make me feel better, and she *needed* to do anything she could to help ease my burden and heartache. Accepting that help, hers and yours, created a lovely connection that I felt with all of you who offered help, and made me feel so cared for and comforted. *Thank you*. There is a lesson in this for all of us. Someday, everybody needs help. If you haven't already faced a crisis that disrupts your life, most likely you someday will. And, I hope you will remember that your friends and family that love you *want* to help, and they *need* to help. So, let them— and realize that they will want to do for you as you did for us— *please* pay it forward.

I'd also like to thank Harry's parents for being at the hospital every single day. From the first morning, to Harry's release on September 4th, Harry's parents spent as much time as possible at the hospital. I know it was physically and emotionally exhausting for them, but they never complained. They always showed up with a positive attitude and graciously welcomed every visitor, doctor, nurse and therapist that Harry had. How grateful

I am to have had my very own medical expert and advisor in Harry's brother, Bill. All of Harry's brothers were at the hospital regularly, too, and the whole family took turns talking to his silent form, praying for him, rubbing his feet and hands, touching his face, and of course, running their fingers through his gorgeous hair! I know those were the toughest forty-four days of their lives, but their love and devotion never wavered in the midst of their fear and exhaustion.

Of course, I want to once again thank all of *you* for everything you did to make those days of uncertainty bearable, and at times downright pleasant. You always seemed to know just what we needed! Sometimes, it was a most timely email, phone message, or guestbook entry. Sometimes, one of you would show up with a beautiful goody basket with treats and drinks. At times, there were flowers brought that lifted everyone's spirits. And, the visits themselves were something so important to us— the support you showed, the hugs you gave, the kind words and stories you shared, your physical presence showing support—it all strengthened Harry's family, Harrison and me. And, it helped our medical staff to understand the type of man their patient was, and the impact he had on his friends and colleagues.

Harry and I both want to thank Harrison. It's been a pleasure for me to share with Harry many stories about Harrison's strength and bravery during the hospital stay. Dealing with the near-zero odds of Harry's survival was difficult for everyone, but for a fourteen-year-old son, it had to be devastatingly frightening. It's inspirational that he handled everything with amazing fortitude and strength. He readily stepped into the role of Man of the House, juggling the extra demands of responsibilities and independence with grace and respectability. He never missed a football practice, because he wanted to honor his commitment to his coaches and teammates. I know there were times when the last thing he wanted to do was leave Harry's bedside, but he did it—and he did it knowing that Harry would want him to do so. He told me that no matter how tough 'two-a-day' football practices were, they were nothing compared to the fight that Harry was waging! He was an enormous source of support for me and for his grandparents, aunts, uncles and cousins. Once

Harry came home, Harrison continued to help out in every way possible—walking with Harry, helping with household chores, giving lots of important hugs, just hanging out with and watching over Harry every chance he got. To this day, his love and devotion and reverent appreciation for his family hasn't lessened in the least. It was a very difficult way for a young man to learn how fragile life can be, but I have no doubt that the lessons learned from this have had a very positive impact on him, in ways that will be with him for his entire life. H-Man—thank you! You were a bright shining star of hope and inspiration for us. I wouldn't want to imagine going through that nightmare without you by my side. Dad and I love you beyond description!!

Thank you to our wonderful medical staff. I know most of you never expected Harry to survive, because many of you have told us so. You do this day after day—you save lives, make life easier for the loved ones, then get up the next day and do it again. Forty-four days is a relatively small percentage of a person's life, but your contribution in that time has left an indelible mark on us and a place in our hearts ... forever.

And finally—thank you, God, for answering our prayers.

We are on the home stretch—returning to normal life, and so very grateful to be in this state of improvement, health, and happiness in less than eight months since that disastrous first day back in late July. Here's to Harry for coming back to us, and for doing what is necessary to stay with us for many more years to come.

And, here's to all of you—for your love, support and friendship.

Thank you!
The Whites

Months after Harry was released from the hospital, someone asked me if I was bitter or resentful about everything that had happened. I didn't hesitate with my answer and I feel as strongly about this now as I did then. Not only am I not bitter or resentful, I am GRATEFUL for all of the good that happened as a result of this. Of course, if the ending hadn't been happy, I might feel differently. The thousands of good things that happened because of those fateful hospital days far outweigh the trials and challenges of those weeks. Some of the benefits are immeasurable. For me alone, this has forever changed me in a positive way.

July 23, 2011

Two Years Later … Celebrating Life

Today is the two-year anniversary of the cardiac event that put me into the hospital. At the risk of diluting the exquisite quality of Cathy's writing of her journal, I feel compelled to send you an update today and to thank each of you for contributing to my recovery.

THIS ONE IS FROM HARRY.…

"I had been alive at my own funeral." That was the feeling that came over me when I awoke from the coma nearly two years ago. As I read the letters and notes and cards and received the calls and personal good wishes, as the fog slowly cleared and I was told what had happened starting at 5:30 a.m. on July 23, 2009, and as I read Cathy's CaringBridge journal that so eloquently describes each day's events and the roller coaster of emotions that accompanied the descent to near death and the slow, miraculous ascent to consciousness and life, I was overwhelmed by the outpouring of palpable love from so many wonderful, thoughtful people.

Upon reflection, it is truly remarkable. People said things and wrote things that they probably would not have, had death not been so imminent. Boxes filled with hundreds of written messages are saved and will be treasured for the rest of my life … a tangible silver lining to these harrowing events.

Others want to know how all of this altered my perspective about life. The changes were many and they were monumental.

The most significant change was in my relationship with beautiful Cathy. Before July 2009, I thought I loved her as much as I could; but the tenderness and love and understanding and confidence she displayed during the forty-four days in the hospital and throughout the many months of recovery that have followed are simply astounding. When I express my thanks and admiration to her, she shrugs modestly and says, "I just did what I had to do." But who do you know that could've handled all the moving parts of that situation so gracefully, efficiently and lovingly? I thought I loved her completely before; but the love I have for my beautiful, caring, intelligent, sweet Cathy today is unprecedented.

This summer adventure also changed my relationship with young Harrison. I gained a great deal of respect for him as I learned the manner in which he handled the entire event, especially when the doctors thought I wouldn't make it. He showed such strength and courage and he helped his mom when things looked very bleak. As a result, I treasure every moment with that boy. I know the window is closing, that two years from now he will be off to college and gone from our home. So for right now I want to see every football practice and every baseball game and sit with my arm around him as we watch a movie at home eating popcorn together. **I understand better the value of savoring every moment in our lives.**

So many others played such a significant role in my barely hanging on and eventual recovery and it seemed each played a specific and critical role. My brother, Bill, the physician, and his wife Kathi, worked tirelessly side-by-side with Cathy to advocate with the treating doctors on my behalf. Bill used his knowledge and expertise to guide the teams of doctors and help them think through various procedures completely.

The White family, my parents and brothers and their families, kept a steady vigil for all forty-four days in my hospital room, even for the days and weeks that I was not conscious. The Grewe family visited regularly but they also filled the role of tending the home front. They did all the things around the house that Cathy was unable to do as she spent all those days and nights with me in ICU. They fed and walked the dogs, did grocery shopping, got the mail and answered calls. They did all of the many tasks that came up at home so that Cathy did not have to do them when she arrived home from the hospital late at night.

And, my extended family and friends ... Please know how much your prayers and letters, your thoughts, Roger's song "Harry's Smile," your photos and posters mean to me. Know for sure that without your individual and collective support, I would not be here.

People ask me regularly how I am doing now on this second anniversary of the ambulance ride to the ER. I feel so much better, this being a year after the last surgery to repair abdominal damage from the procedures in 2009. I'm still pretty sore throughout the trunk of my body, both internally and externally. It's kind of like I've been used as the heavy bag in a boxing training studio. But I am continuing to get better and I am working hard to improve more. I am able to hike and run and mountain bike. I take a spin class a couple times each week and lift weights twice a week as well. It's all physical therapy recommended for best recovery. I was even able to swing a golf club this week, for the first time in a couple of years.

I thank each of you for what you have given to me and my family. Your love, your support, your encouragement, your continued prayers—these are personal treasures given so generously when we needed them most. Before this event, I didn't know how many of you felt. I do now and for that knowledge of the love you expressed for me and my family, I consider myself a very fortunate man. Your outpouring of allegiance and affection will be treasured to the end of my days on this earth. I thank you with all of my healthy heart.
Harry

"Harry, It is so good to hear from you in this forum. I wanted you to know that, as I also approach my two-year anniversary of my experience, I am also extremely grateful for all of the people who gave me support and inspiration, including you. Your visit at the hospital was a catalyst for my attitude about recovery and for that I thank you.
Just to let you know, my son and I returned yesterday from a ten-day golf trip to Scotland. It was a magical experience, one I would not have been able to make without people like you. Many thanks and God bless,"
Hank

July 30, 2015

From Harrison

Six years ago today.

The only question on my mind as I tried to force myself to sleep was whether or not I would still have a father when I woke the next morning. That horrible thought was the last one to drift through my mind every night for the horrendous weeks that followed. The phone call came in at 11:30 p.m.— never a good sign. In the brutal and painstakingly long hours that followed, my dad would experience complete cardiac failure and the life would slowly but surely leave his body.

After forty-five minutes of increasingly hopeless CPR and an out of body experience, nobody expected the miracle that followed. In a true act of God, my dad was sent back to my mom and me.

Dad, you are, in every sense of the word, my hero. You take on each and every day with a grace and determination that I have never seen in anyone else. Your positive, uplifting spirit is a blessing and a pleasure to be around. You have mentored me through two decades of life, teaching me some of life's most difficult lessons with strength and ease. Words cannot express how incredibly thankful I am to have you here with me. The perspective I gained from having a glimpse of life without you was invaluable. But, beyond that, the opportunity to have a chance to show you how much you mean to me after knowing what life would be like without you is one that very few people ever have. I feel so lucky to have that perspective and to have had the second chance of showing you just how much you're loved.

I, along with many, many others am incredibly lucky to have you in my life. I am proud to call you my father. I love you more than words can express. Dad, here's to you!

Harrison White

In the years since the "Summer Adventure of 2009," Harry has had many opportunities to share what we learned from this experience. Sometimes, it's just a conversation over dinner with friends, sometimes his perspective has been shared with a bigger audience. Always, the reception is warm and welcoming and listeners leave shaking their heads in awe and I believe, feeling inspired.

In the summer of 2010, Harry and I traveled to Colorado to visit with Bill and Kathi. It was wonderful to be with them, to celebrate life together, and to reflect back on how close we came to not being able to enjoy that time together with the four of us. We attended a service at Bill and Kathi's church and after the service, Harry spoke to a group of parishioners. In his talk, he shared the scenario of those days of hospitalization and the stories of his out-of-body experiences. He thanked everyone for their support and prayers. Many of them, without ever having met Harry had prayed for him constantly. He stressed that it was difficult for him to come back to life on earth, because it was so wonderful *THERE*. He explained that he is not afraid of death, because he has had a glimpse of how incredibly beautiful the next phase is. He encouraged everyone to not worry about death, theirs or a loved one's, and to accept it not only as a part of life, but as a stepping stone to a perfect life of peace and happiness. His talk was met with silent awe and many tears.

After he finished, several people came up to him to thank him and to express their relief that he had survived such an ordeal. One woman in particular, with tears streaming down her face, told Harry in a trembling voice that she had just lost her mother six weeks before. She explained that she had been feeling betrayed, by God and by her religion and that she had not been back to church since her mother died. She explained that some unknown source had compelled her to come back to church that particular morning. She didn't at all want to, but forced herself to go. After hearing Harry talk, she said she felt like a huge weight had been lifted from her shoulders. For the past six weeks, she had been afraid for her mother, and angry at God for taking her. Over the half hour that Harry spoke, her attitude completely changed to that of peace, that she now felt that her mother was in a better place and that she was no longer suffering. She said she was certain now that she would again someday be with her.

In April of 2013, Harry was honored to receive a Men of Character Award from the Boy Scouts of America. His acceptance speech centered around the gratefulness he feels at a second chance to live and from the many blessings that came about from those awful days of the summer of 2009. He again shocked his audience with the story of his battle for survival. When he told the stories of his out-of-body experiences, the room was silent and still and the audience amazement was palpable.

In October of 2016, Harry was a selected speaker at his forty-five-year Stanford University reunion. The prompt for this Class Panel discussion was "What will bring us the most happiness in the last third of our lives?" Harry's perspective about life, love, family and friends, one that was shaped by the summer of 2009, gave him many thoughts to share. In his speech, Harry outlined the events of those fateful summer days to the amazement of everyone in the audience. He cited these special circumstances as leading to the advice he was about to give to them.

Harry's advice was three-fold. He advised his classmates to first consider starting each day with a clean slate, to prioritize the must-dos and obligations by keeping them in perspective. He encouraged them to replace some of the obligations of their everyday lives with more things that they wanted to do, and to focus on their to-do lists as if they didn't have much time left on earth.

This led to his second tidbit of advice, which was a focus on family and friends. He urged everyone to vocalize their love and appreciation for the people who mean the most. He encouraged his audience to spend time with their favorite people, to create memories and enjoy the precious days left in their lives. Harry understands that the cultivation and nurturing of relationships makes us happy, brings us joy and improves the quality of our lives. He specifically suggested doing something each day … a little thing, a small gesture to make life better for the most important person in one's life. He also suggested doing something randomly for someone in order to make their day better. These are not just words in his speech … Harry does all of this himself.

Harry's final bit of advice was about exiting from this life. He urged his audience to not be fearful, but to see the end of life as a transition to one of unimaginable beauty and peace. He knows … he is 100 percent convinced that he was "there" and that it was magnificent.

One story that Harry always includes in his talks is about when he was in "limbo," somewhere between life and death, perhaps, during his hospital stay. He speaks in vivid detail about going to his grandmother's house in Montana (his grandmother passed away in 1976).

As he approaches the screen door, he can smell chocolate chip cookies baking and as he looks through the door, he notices every detail. His grandmother is at the stove, with her back to him. He notices everything about the room. The floor tile is black and white twelve-inch tiles. The formica countertops and kitchen table are lemon yellow edged in shiny silver-ridged steel. He sees where everything is—the stove, the sink, the window, the refrigerator, the door. When he later asks his mother about the kitchen, she confirms that every detail is spot on and this is the house where she grew up.

Here is his beloved grandmother, working at the stove with an apron on. Everything about the scene smells and looks ... *heavenly*. He always had a special connection with her and wanted so badly to go sit at her kitchen table, to chat with her and have cookies and milk. Just one more time, he wants her to put her hand on his face and to laugh with him, then sweetly tell him how much she adores him. Instead, she turns slowly from the stove, smiles softly, almost sadly at him and says,

"Don't come in, Harry. We're not ready for you yet."

Epilogue

Some time during Harry's 44-day ordeal, I promised myself that I would eventually write a book about what had happened to him and to our family. There were many significant stories that I didn't have time to post on CaringBridge as those days were already so busy. I hoped that a book would give more people opportunities to read about Harry's ordeal and to be inspired by the lessons of those events. There are so many people in this world dealing with significant challenges. Stories like Harry's do much to boost the spirits and hopefulness of surviving those challenges. Sharing that hope and faith and inspiring that in others was my purpose in writing about that summer.

It's now more than twelve years since Harry came home from the hospital. Four years after that summer, Harrison graduated from high school and went on to play baseball at Yale University. With both of us being retired, Harry and I had the freedom and the privilege of being able to travel to almost every single one of Harrison's games. After college graduation, in 2017, the Miami Marlins drafted Harrison and he had a successful career in the minor leagues for two years. We also saw most of those games. In those six years, not a day went by when I failed to give thanks for Harry's survival and subsequent health. I cannot even begin to imagine not having Harry around for the amazing journey of those six magical, unforgettable years. Now, Harrison is applying to medical school. Becoming a patient care physician was something that always interested him, but after the summer of 2009, it became his calling.

In 2017, when Luke Bryan's song "Most People are Good" came out, it immediately made me think of those 44 days that Harry spent in ICU. Over and over again I was struck by how good people were. From our closest friends and relatives to complete strangers, we were surrounded by such incredible *goodness*. It was one of the many great lessons of a story that thankfully had a happy ending. Even now, twelve years later, I still feel surrounded by the warmth of all of the amazing support during that difficult summer and I still give thanks for the inherent goodness of people.

The lessons I learned from Harry's "adventure" have not diminished over the past years. Instead, they have become even more vivid and important to me, and to Harry and to Harrison as the years go by. We frequently talk together about the impact that that summer had on us. We are all painfully aware that life is precious and can change in an instant. We have become more patient and forgiving, as we think about the possibilities of difficulties that people around us are enduring. We tell family members and friends how much we love them and appreciate them, knowing that someday, we may no longer have the chance to share those sentiments. Our spirituality and faith have grown, knowing that we have been genuine recipients of answered prayers. We are eternally grateful for how this ordeal helped our friends. Many have told us they strive to be better parents, more loving and forgiving spouses, more understanding, engaging children and more supportive siblings, as a result of the change of perspective they felt after witnessing Harry's fight for survival.

Kenny Chesney's song, "I'm Alive" has become our White Family Theme Song. In the summer of 2022, when we see Kenny Chesney in concert, you can be sure we will be standing, holding hands and singing along … with every word!

So damn easy to say that life's so hard
Everybody's got their share of battle scars
As for me, I'd like to thank my lucky stars
That I'm alive and well
It'd be easy to add up all the pain
And all the dreams you sat and watched go up in flames
Dwell on the wreckage as it smolders in the rain
But not me, I'm alive.
Stars are dancin' on the water here tonight
It's good for the soul and there's not a soul in sight
This boat has caught its wind and brought me back to life
Now I'm alive and well.
And today, you know, that's good enough for me
Breathing in and out's a blessing, can't you see
Today's the first day of the rest of my life
And I'm alive and well
Yeah, I'm alive and well.

ACKNOWLEDGEMENTS

Thank you to all of you who encouraged me to write this book. Whether it was "You should write a book someday!" or "How is the book coming along?" or "I can't wait to read your book. I'll be first in line to buy it!"; all of your comments encouraged me to keep going on what was at times a very emotional, difficult endeavor. Harry and I went through boxes of tissue in the dozens of times that we read through the postings in the manuscript and re-lived those days. Thankfully, the last several sets of tears were happy ones.

Thank you to all of you CaringBridge contributors and email friends, our fabulous support team members from all over the world. Each and every one of you is a key element in the story, a story that most likely wouldn't have had the same outcome without you.

Thank you to David Welday of HigherLife Publishing. Your warmth and kindness are matched by your professionalism and efficiency and it's all very much appreciated. You and your staff have made this process not only seamless but pleasurable as well. I especially thank you for your intuitiveness in matching me with my project manager, Julie Castro.

Thank you, Julie Castro, for guiding me through this experience so well with great ideas, tips, advice and support. You have graciously, thoroughly, and patiently answered every one of my "naïve author" questions. Kudos to David for partnering us. You and I "get each other" and communicating with you is as easy as if we had been friends for decades. Although we have never met face-to-face, I would know you if I saw you on the street and I would immediately give you a big hug. This working relationship and friendship were meant to be, were they not? I can't imagine a better publishing experience than to be in your loving, guiding hands. I'm quite certain that our bond will continue long after the book duties are done and I look forward to that!

Thank you to my editor, Jennifer Burdge. You are so good! I am in awe of your knowledge and efficiency. You are indeed the dream study-buddy for anyone taking an English or Grammar course! I especially appreciate your personal thoughts and ideas about Harrison's letter and other suggestions that you had. You evaluate and consider the entire project, the storyline itself, not just the punctuation and grammar.

Thank you to the entire crew at HigherLife Publishing! There have been so many wonderful, professional contributions to this project, by project managers, editors, typesetters, cover designers, and more. I can't tell you how much I appreciate every effort made on behalf of *Back From Code Blue*. Special thanks go to my cover designer, Jonathan Lewis of Jonlin Creative and my typesetter, Faithe Thomas of Master Design Marketing.

Thank you to my friends who took the time to quickly read my book and to write an endorsement. Tom Lallas, Jeff Reuter, Blaine Hammond, Sandy Barker and Chris Griffith, I thank you all for your immediate, enthusiastic responses that you would be willing to make your busy days even busier by reading my manuscript. Your friendship and support mean the world to me.

I was saddened to see how many friends who posted beautiful messages on CaringBridge have since passed away. How I wish you were all still here to see your words honored in print and so that you could understand how precious those notes will always be to us. Harry and I have lost six family members since that fateful summer; our sister-in-law, Maggie; our nephew, Trent; both of Harry's parents, Harry and Helen; my mom, Catherine; and Harry's brother, Bob. I am heartbroken that you are not here to receive our thanks in person and in print. You fulfilled your roles of love and support every minute of every day that summer and for that, Harry and I cannot thank you enough.

For our family members who are still with us ... my dad, Carl, Rick, Robyn, Garrett, Rolly, Bill, Kathi, Jim, Alexandria, Natalie, and Taylor; I thank you for your support that hasn't lessened since those awful days following July 23, 2009. I said it earlier in the book ... I don't know how people make it through catastrophes without the support of their loved ones. Thank you!

Thank you to the members of the band, Back from Blue. Who knew back in the autumn of 2009, when you became a band, that the name of your band would inspire the name of my book?! I can't thank you enough for your brilliance and creativity and for giving our family some really wonderful memories of those years when you were together and performing so beautifully. Back from Blue ... Austin, Melissa, Chandler,

Sebastian, Jason and Harrison; I thank you all for inspiring a title that, to me, says it all.

Harrison ... Those days in 2009 were horrible for us both, yet they were also very sweet and tender in that we spent a lot of time together forging on as a team through the hours and days. I wanted Dad to live for you as much as I wanted him to live for me, and your strong, sweet, powerful presence kept me going hour after hour and kept me fighting for his survival. Your smiles and laughter were exactly what I needed to get me through some difficult moments. Your incredible strength amazed me every day. I can only imagine how frightened you were and how many emotions you kept inside. No matter what happened during the day, holding your hand as you fell asleep at night always made me peaceful and made me believe that Dad would survive. Since those horrible days, you have done nothing but make us both proud of the fine young man you have become. Your strength, compassion, character and integrity have continued to be admirable year after year. I cannot begin to thank you enough for your love and inspiration in those days of 2009 and for your constant support since then in my writing this book.

Harry, YOU are the reason that this enormous community of friends, family members, colleagues, neighbors, patients, acquaintances and even strangers begged God to spare your life. I believe that this group of supporters who know you would agree with me. We need more people like you on earth, not fewer. There is something so wrong, so unacceptable about losing a human being with exceptional, admirable qualities at a young age. When you were close to losing your life, it was as if our community was "offended" at the thought of losing someone who still had so much to give and contribute. It was unacceptable! It was sobering as well. If this could happen to you, it could happen to anyone.

New friends and acquaintances know you to be friendly, warm, genuine, caring, humorous and charismatic. Your friends who know you better see even more of your admirable qualities; your generosity, integrity, selflessness, positive attitude, your leadership of our family, your commitment to doing what is right, your accountability and the good character examples that you set.

Is it any wonder that our community was not ready to lose one of their best at such a young age? When it was apparent that you would survive, I believe we all heaved a sigh of relief and felt that, again, everything was right with the world.

Thank you, for so strongly fighting your toughest fight to come back to all of us! I love you, Miracle Man!

About the Author

Cathy Grewe White was born in Richfield, Minnesota in 1954, coincidentally in the same hospital, and in the same year as one of Harry's four brothers. When she was eight, she moved with her parents and brother, Rick, to Arcadia, California where she grew up and attended Arcadia High School. At USC School of Dentistry in 1976, she met Harry as he was completing his orthodontic residency.

Harry was born in Black Eagle, Montana, then moved to Minnesota with his parents and four brothers, Rolly, Bill, Bob and Jim. They then moved to the San Fernando Valley in California, where Harry's father worked as Vice President of Western Airlines in Los Angeles. Harry attended Chaminade High School, then went on to Stanford University, earning a degree in Honors Humanities. He attended dental school at the University of Oregon Health Sciences Center in Portland, and returned to Southern California for his orthodontic education. He spent the summer of 1974 as a Naval officer working as a dentist for the U.S. Indian Health Service, living and working on the reservation in Belcourt, North Dakota.

Cathy loves to cook, entertain and travel. She is an avid football and baseball fan. She has a passion for architectural and space design. She loves creative crafts and enjoys sewing, knitting, jewelry making and scrapbooking. She has been a member of the Mensa Society since 1985.

While Harry was practicing orthodontics, he enjoyed teaching at USC and giving board certification courses to other orthodontists throughout the U. S. and Canada. In 1985, he earned his private pilot license. A talented athlete, he played baseball at Stanford University and has enjoyed playing several sports since his Stanford days. He won many tennis tournaments over the years, and now plays golf and pickle ball. He is a certified scuba diver and also enjoys biking and hiking. He joins Cathy as an avid baseball and football fan. Harry especially enjoyed the years of coaching Little League, flag football, golf and school baseball while Harrison was in middle school and he proved himself to be an exceptional, inspirational coach. Harry continues to be active in Stanford Alumni activities, helping plan and facilitate events at reunions. Harry does a great job as the White Family social chairman.

To connect with the author, please contact her at cathywhite07@ gmail.com.